Crochet for Absolute Beginners

Learn to Crochet in 2-Weeks or Less!
Kit, Stiches, Abbreviations, Symbols, Patterns
& Project Ideas with Step-by-step Pictures
and Illustrations

By

YVONNE CHAMBERS

© Copyright 2023 by (Yvonne Chambers) - All rights reserved.

This document is geared towards providing exact and reliable information in regard to the topic and issue covered. The publication is sold with the idea that the publisher is not required to render accounting, officially permitted, or otherwise, qualified services. If advice is necessary, legal, or professional, a practiced individual in the profession should be ordered.

- From a Declaration of Principles, which was accepted and approved equally by a Committee of the American Bar Association and a Committee of Publishers and Associations. In no way is it legal to reproduce, duplicate, or transmit any part of this document in either electronic means or in printed format. Recording of this publication is strictly prohibited, and any storage of this document is not allowed unless with written permission from the publisher. All rights reserved. The information provided herein is stated to be truthful and consistent, in that any liability, in terms of inattention or otherwise, by any usage or abuse of any policies, processes, or directions contained within is the solitary and utter responsibility of the recipient reader. Under no circumstances will any legal responsibility or blame be held against the publisher for any reparation, damages, or monetary loss due to the information herein, either directly or indirectly. Respective authors own all copyrights not held by the publisher. The information herein is offered for informational purposes solely and is universal as so. The presentation of the information is without contract or any type of guarantee assurance. The trademarks that are used are without any consent, and the publication of the trademark is without permission or backing by the trademark owner. All trademarks and brands within this book are for clarifying purposes only and are owned by the owners themselves, not affiliated with this document.

TABLE OF CONTENTS

Introduction 1

Chapter 1: Equipment For Crochet 3

    1.1 A Crochet Hook's Anatomy 3

    1.2 Measurements for Crochet Hooks 5

    1.3 Crochet Hooks: How To Hold Them 9

    1.4 Stitch Markers, Row Counters, And Shears 10

    1.5 Macrame Board 12

    1.6 Scissors 14

    1.7 Adhesives 15

    1.8 Cords 15

    1.9 Metal Comb 16

    1.10 Tree Branch 17

    1.11 Yarns 17

    1.12 Hooks 18

    1.13 Wool Needles 18

    1.14 Stitch Makers 18

    1.15 Anti-corrosion pins 19

    1.16 Project bag 19

    1.17 Notebook and pen 19

    1.18 The needle and thread for sewing 19

    1.19 Protective goggles and facemasks 19

1.20 Spray on Some Starch..20

1.21 Stuffing for Toys...20

1.22 Felt and Fabric Pieces 21

Chapter 2: How To Choose The Appropriate Yarn 22

2.1 Yarn Fibers..22

2.2 Yarn Weight..23

2.3 Gauge..24

2.4 The Yarn Label 26

2.5 Different Yarn For Crochet and Their Use 27

2.6 Types of Yarn..31

2.7 Merino Wool 33

2.8 Wool 34

2.9 Alpaca Yarn 36

2.10 Angora Yarn 37

2.11 Cashmere Yarn...39

2.12 Silk Yarn..41

2.13 Silky Soy Yarn..44

2.14 Cotton Yarn 45

2.15 Hemp Yarn 47

2.16 Bamboo Yarn..49

2.17 Linen Yarn 51

2.18 Acrylic Yarn..53

Chapter 3: Crochet Stitches, Abbreviations, and Symbols 55

3.1 Chain Stitch 55

3.2 Slip Stitch 56

3.3 Single crochet stitch.. 57

3.4 Double Stitch Crochet 59

3.5 The Half Double Crochet Stitch 63

3.6 Treble Crochet Stitch 64

3.7 Stitch In The Sand 66

3.8 Double Crochet 2 OR 3 Together 68

3,9 Cluster Stitch 69

3.10 Shell Stitch 70

3.11 Stitches in the Front and Back of the Post 71

3.12 Increases.. 73

3.13 Decreases 73

3.14 Crochet Stitches Worked Around a Circle 74

3.15 Alterations In Color 76

3.16 Techniques For Safely Weaving in Tails 79

3.17 Correct Crochet Hook Grip 80

Chapter 4: Patterns 89

1. Cable 89

2. The Cabbage Patch (n.) 91

3. Hotcross Bun 93

4. The Numbers Zero and Crosses 97

5. Triangles Turned Inside Out 100

Chapter 5: Projects 104

1. Hairpin Lace Neck Scarf 104

2. Broomstick Lace Jewelry Frame 107

3. Freeform Handbag..112

4. Polish Star Pillow 114

5. Bruges Lace 125

Conclusion.. **130**

Introduction

In the needlework technique known as crochet, a fabric is fashioned from loops of yarn using a hook instead of a needle. Using crochet, one may create a wide variety of items, including but not limited to blankets, scarves, caps, and sweaters. Although the exact date and location of the invention of crochet are unknown, it is generally agreed that the craft was first practiced in China or Arabia. The kind of crochet practice now made its way to Europe in the 1800s, and its popularity there has only increased since then. The trade of crochet is very adaptable, and it may be used to make a vast range of different things. Dishcloths, discovers, hats, and scarves are some of the most common crocheted items. Other popular items include blankets and scarves. Nevertheless, you are allowed to purchase these goods! You need a little imagination and some crochet skills to make just about anything you can think of.

Both crochet and knitting are forms of needlework that may be used to make a wide range of products. Some examples of these goods are blankets, caps, and scarves. The primary distinction between knitting and crochet is that knitting is done with two needles, whereas crocheting is done with a single hook. If you have never done crochet before, you will become an expert by following the straightforward instructions in this book, which explain each process stage in easy-to-understand detail.

It is possible to construct intriguing stitch patterns by combining the fundamental stitches in various ways. It can achieve various diverse effects; stitch patterns may be lacey or solid, multi-coloured or monochrome, patterned or plain.

If this is your first time trying your hand at crocheting, you may be curious about whether or not it's a worthwhile hobby and whether or not you have the necessary skill set to get started. Does one need a certain level of skill to crochet?

The answer to that question is NO! There is absolutely no need for any specialized ability. You possess the necessary skill set as well.

The encouraging thing is that almost anybody can learn to crochet. Crochet is done by individuals of all ages, from very small toddlers to elderly people. Both men and women do crochet. People from all over the globe do crocheting. Crocheting is a craft practiced by persons with impairments, including the blind. Everyone, regardless of socioeconomic status, crochets at some point.

You won't have a hard time getting started crocheting since there are a few obstacles standing in your way, but there are a few things you should think about before you begin.

Chapter 1:
Equipment For Crochet

To get started crocheting, you actually don't need too much material to work with. An excellent collection of hooks, a reliable pair of scissors, and some clip-on stitch markers are all you need to get started crocheting. In this chapter, we will discuss the crochet hook, the various types of hooks that are available today, and the proper way to hold the hook.

1.1 A Crochet Hook's Anatomy

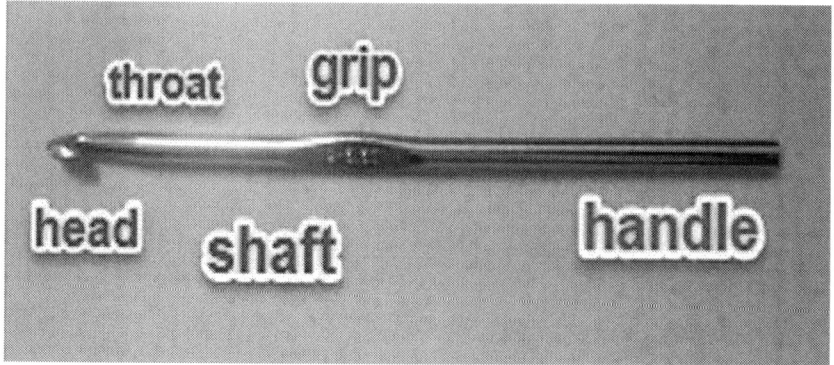

The majority of crochet hooks are made using the same construction method. The length of the handle can be adjusted; however, the majority of hooks are either five or seven inches long. The piece of the handle that has been smoothed out is called the grip, and this is where you will grab the hook in order to exert control over it. As you work your way up to the head of the hook, you will first come across the shaft of the hook, followed by the neck of the hook, and finally, the head of the hook. The length of the neck and the form of the hook head are the primary factors that differentiate one type of hook from another, in addition to the material—aluminum, plastic, wood, or bamboo, for example—that is used to manufacture the hook.

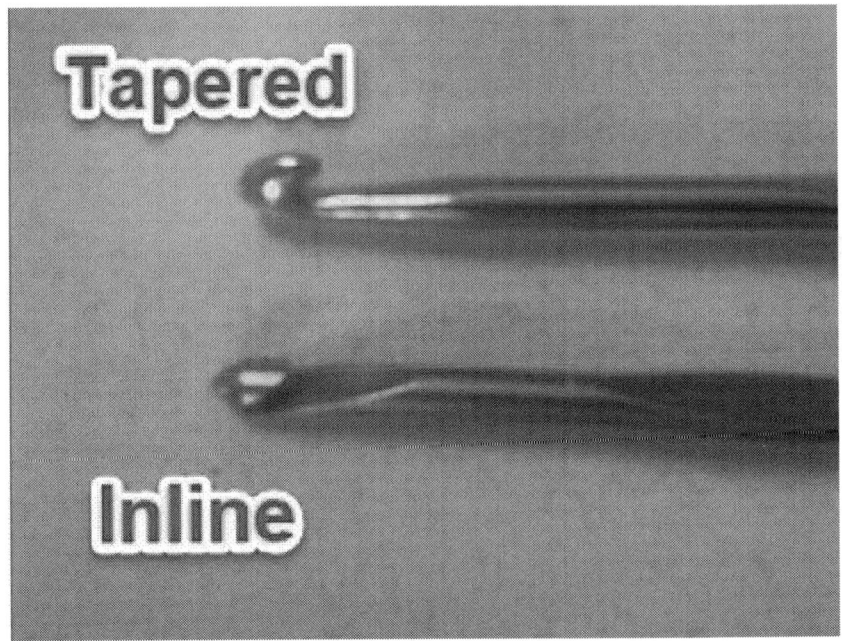

Inline hooks have a head that is more angular and pointed than other types of hooks. Hook heads on tapered hooks are more rounded and smoother than those on other types of hooks. The two distinct types of heads both result in identical stitches; therefore, the decision of which type to use comes down to personal preference. Some crocheters prefer inline hooks (like Susan Bates hooks) because they consider they have a better grasp on the yarn than tapered hooks (like Boye hooks), while other crocheters prefer tapered hooks (like Boye hooks) because they believe they don't splinter the yarn in addition to inline hooks. Examine all of the options to see which one suits your needs best. Additionally, there are crochet hooks available with padded handles. These handles can be fashioned from polymer clay that has been baked, plastic, or even big ergonomic handles designed specifically for individuals who have difficulty grasping a crochet hook.

1.2 Measurements for Crochet Hooks

Letters and numbers are frequently used in the United States as a means of indicating the sizes of crochet hooks. For example, I/9 is one of my most often used hook sizes (5.50mm). It is common practice to recommend hook sizes ranging from E/4 (3/5 mm) through K/10 12 (13 mm) (6.5mm). On the other hand, you might come encounter hooks that just mention the dimensions in millimeters. By utilizing this helpful advice, you can ensure that you are using the appropriate hook size for the pattern you are working on.

US Size	Millimeter Size
B/1	2.25mm
C/2	2.75mm
D/3	3.25mm
E/4	3.5mm
F/5	3.75mm
G/6	4mm
7	4.5mm
H/8	5mm
I/9	5.5mm
J/10	6mm
K/10 ½	6.5mm
L/11	8mm
M-N/13	9mm
N-P/15	10mm
P/Q	15mm
Q	16mm
S	19mm

It's possible that the hooks you find are measured in either metric or British/Canadian systems of measurement. The number of barbs on US hooks is directly proportionate to the size of the US hook. Millimeters are used to measure hook sizes, and a US I/9 (5.50mm) is roughly equivalent to a size 5 in the United Kingdom and Canada. Utilizing this chart, you will be able to convert sizes from the United States to those used in the United Kingdom and Canada.

US Sizes	Metric Sizes	UK/Canadian
0	2.0	14
1	2.25	13
2	2.75	12
-	3.0	11
3	3.25	10
4	3.50	-
5	3.75	9
6	4.0	8
7	4.5	7
8	5.0	6
9	5.5	5
10	6.0	4
10 ½	6.5	3
-	7.0	2
-	7.5	1
11	8.0	0
13	9.0	00
15	10.0	000
17	12.0	-
19	16.0	-
35	19.0	-

Steel Crochet Hooks

Crocheting with thread requires the use of steel hooks, which have very small heads on their hooks. Hooks made of steel are a different size than hooks made of other materials. The lower the number, the more prominent the hook will be. Some stainless-steel hooks are so delicate that their point is almost as acute as that of a needle.

STEEL CROCHET HOOK CONVERSION		
Metric (mm)	US	UK
3.5	00	-
3.25	0	0
2.75	1	1
2.25	2	1 1/2
2.1	3	2
2.0	4	2 1/2
1.9	5	3
1.8	6	3 1/2
1.65	7	4
1.5	8	4 1/2
1.4	9	5
1.3	10	5 1/2
1.1	11	6
1.0	12	6 1/2
.85	13	7
.75	14	-

Hooks for Tunisian crochet

Because of this, Tunisian crochet hooks, which are often referred to as Afghan hooks, are an awful lot longer than their normal counterparts. This is because when you crochet in the Tunisian technique, you hold the stitches on the hook as you work across the forward pass, and then you work them off the hook as you come back across the row. The reason for this is so that you may create more space between the stitches. You can get hooks that are long and single, as well as hooks that have cables that are used to attach the stitches. Both types of hooks are available.

1.3 Crochet Hooks: How To Hold Them

When it relates to how to properly hold the hook, the "pencil hold" and the "knife hold" are the two most common ways of thinking about it. That its name suggests, the pencil hold entails grasping the hook in the same manner as one would a pencil. When using the knife hold, you should grasp the hook as though you were going to use a kitchen knife to cut a piece of food. It is a matter of personal choice as to which hold you employ because both holds will result in the same number of stitches for you. Take advantage of the option that makes you feel the most at ease. The most of the time when I crochet, I use the pencil hold, but when I'm working with particularly thick yarn, I switch to the knife hold so that I have more flexibility and leverage to draw the yarn through the stitching.

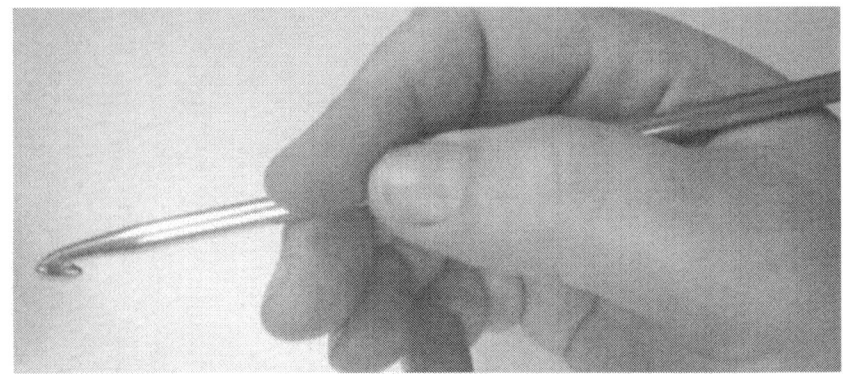
Pencil Hold

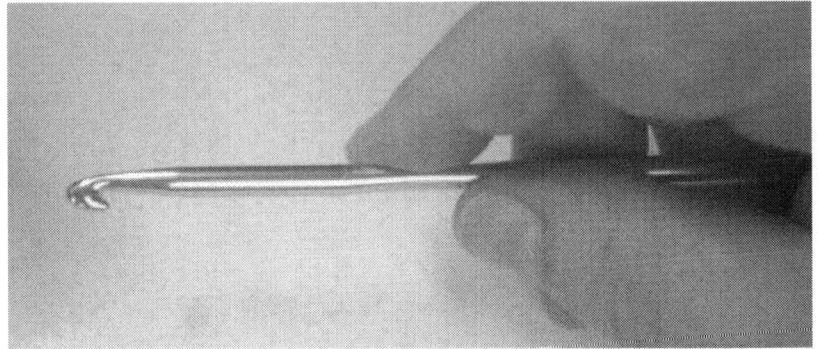
Knife Hold

1.4 Stitch Markers, Row Counters, And Shears

Shears are an essential tool for crochet artists, and they should be of high quality and nice looking. Shears should be used only on yard and thread. Be very careful with your shears, and under no circumstances should you allow anyone to use them on parchment. When you manage to cut yarn or thread with paper, the blades will become dull and the yarn or thread will fray. Additionally, it is essential to have a beautiful set of clip-on stitch markers at your disposal. You can use stitch markers to mark the beginning and end of a pattern repeat, as well as the commencement of a round, and they can also be used to hold your current stitch in place in the event that you need to lay your work down. Row counters can be as straightforward as a sheet of paper and a pen or pencil. Alternatively, you can purchase row counters that are designed to fit over your finger. When you first begin working with charts and graphs, a row counting will be of great assistance to you in staying on track and avoiding being confused.

That is actually all that is required to get started crocheting. As your crocheting expertise grows, you will get familiar with a variety of crochet techniques, including Tunisian and Hairpin Lace, as well as the sorts of hooks that you prefer to use the most. Those of you who are just getting started should put money into an excellent quality collection of aluminum hooks that range in size from E to K. You will get a lot of use out of these throughout the years. Even after all these years of crocheting, I still use the very first set I ever bought.

The abundance of crochet accoutrements that is currently available can be pretty overwhelming; thus, the easiest way to get started is to determine exactly what you want to crochet and then get the supplies and equipment that are required for that project. Because they are simple, entertaining, and gratifying to make, the characters depicted in the book are an excellent place to start learning and perfecting your crochet skills if you are just getting started in the hobby. While each pattern will offer a list of the yarns, needle sizes, and other goods like buttons that are required, you will additionally require certain fundamental equipment like scissors, a wool needle, and toy filling. The following is a list among some basic crochet equipment that will assist you in getting started: Chapter 2: Material and Tools of Macrame

Macramé's practical beginnings can be traced back to when jute, hemp, linen, and other natural fibers were widely used in weaving nets and cloth. Sailors and merchants who ventured to far-flung lands brought back novel supplies that advanced the art and ensured its continuation from one generation to the next.

Now, in the modern era of abundant information available online, you may find the most amazing variety of fabrics, beads, and findings to make anything your heart desires. It's because we now have access to everything mentioned.

Macramé calls far more than the standard fare of yarn, beads, and ornaments. Most of the materials and equipment needed to build the projects detailed in this book are likely already in your possession. Whatever you might be missing can be picked up at a nearby bead shop, craft supply store, or even hardware store.

1.5 Macrame Board

When working on a macramé project, it is necessary to attach the object to a surface, usually using T pins but also with masking tape. With the knots in place and easily managed, working with your cords is streamlined. Macramé boards are available in a wide variety of sizes and shapes at your local bead shop, craft supply store, and even online. Their fiber board design allows them to be around 12 inches by 18 inches in size (30 centimeters by 46 centimeters). Most macramé boards were available to the public, featuring grids on the surface and rulers down the sides. You can take them down if you want to, but I think they provide invaluable direction while I work and, therefore, leave them taped or shrink-wrapped in place. Some even have illustrations showing you how to tie the simple knots you'll need to know to get started with macramé.

If the macramé project you're working on is too big for a standard board, you may need to make your own. Choose a receptive board that will allow you to easily pin your creations.

It's also important to use a surface that won't get damaged from adhering, removing, and repositioning the tape. It has been my experience that larger projects benefit from the surface of an old desk. When I needed to hang a long curtain, I made a wooden board three feet wide and six feet long (91 centimeters by 183 centimeters). Making your macrame surface requires a grid to be drawn and rulers to be added to the edges. Having a piece of measuring tape on hand could also be helpful if you're working on an unusual surface like an airplane tray or a table.

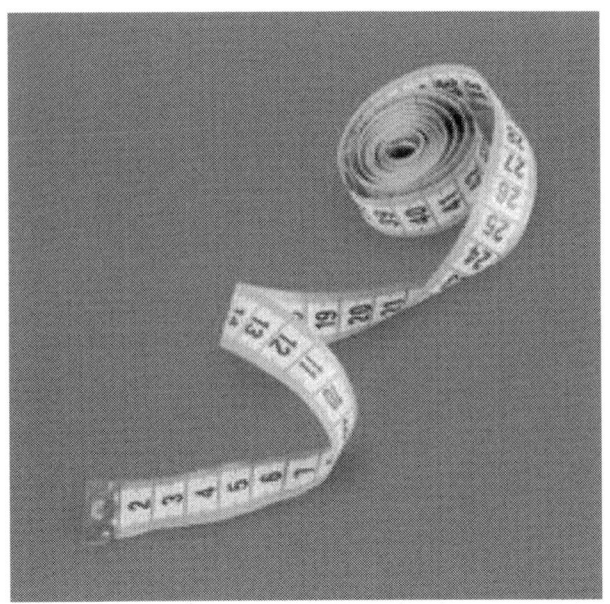

1.6 Scissors

Most macramé projects use thin strands that can be easily cut with a pair of craft scissors, the kind of scissors you probably already own. A pair of little trimming scissors made for sewing would be useful for finishing a job by snipping away any unnecessary length. With them, you can get in close to a knot without risking damaging it as you trim it.

Using suede, leather skin, or string is required for a few of the projects in this book. You'll need a pair of scissors and some serious muscle to cut through those. A pair of wonderful economy shears from a store that specialized in leather products are my go-to set of high-quality scissors for any task. They are small enough to work with the hides, yet powerful enough to cut through tough knots. In addition, they excel at just much everything else you can throw at them. It is recommended that you get a high-quality pair of scissors if you plan on working with these materials frequently.

1.7 Adhesives

The final knot or knots in most macramé projects are secured with glue or some other method. The materials being used will dictate the best adhesive to use.

White glue is highly suggested when working with waxed linen, hemp, cotton, silk, and other fibers. Rubber cement or contact cement is ideal for use on leather and suede. The heart belt buckle features a combination of E-6000 and epoxy, both of which are highly powerful adhesives used to fuse together nonporous objects like wire and labradorite beads. Both of these adhesives require that you work in a well-ventilated area, and you should read and heed all safety labels before beginning use. The Ultimate! is my favorite super glue since it is safe to use around children and pets, it is water-based, and it is both extremely strong and flexible.

It's important to think about the adhesive's toxicity level while making your final decision. Keeping this in mind is crucial if the adhesive will be in contact with human flesh.

1.8 Cords

The essential component of everything; without it, there can be no creation! There is a wide selection of cables available, and the vast majority of tutorials need to include guidance on which one to use. If this is not the case, or if you like to build as you go, a 3mm or 4mm three-ply twist could be a nice place to begin.

1.9 Metal Comb

When brushing out the thread that was used for your macramé plumage and fringes, you will need a comb that is durable. A plastic comb is acceptable and can complete the task at hand, but it is not as efficient as a steel comb and cannot perform the task to the same level of quality. Utilize a steel comb for the most efficient and effective results. A pet comb, on the other hand, will not only help you save time but will also unravel any knots that may have grown along the way.

1.10 Tree Branch

These are necessary components for the macramé wall hangings you are creating. Purchasing wooden dowels could be a good idea if you want the project to have a neat, clean appearance. If, on the other hand, you're trying for a more bohemian and rustic appearance, then tree branches or even driftwood will be an excellent choice. Keep an eye out the next time you stroll in the woods or by the water to see if you can find any bits of driftwood or unique tree branches to bring home with you.

1.11 Yarns

The vast majority of the patterns are constructed using only two varieties of yarn: DK (B-ply) and 4-ply (tinkering) yarn. The weight and yardage requirements are specified in each individual pattern. You can use any yarn of a similar weight, but keep in mind that this may change the size of your character [and don't forget to check the yardage before you start, to ensure that you have enough yarn to finish your project.] You can use any yarn of a similar weight, but keep in mind that this may change the size of your character.

1.12 Hooks

There are many different varieties of crochet hooks, including those made of bamboo, steel, aluminum, plastic, or a combination of wood and metal. Some crochet hooks have chunky handles and are ergonomically designed to reduce the risk of experiencing pain when crocheting. It is essential to select a hook that provides a pleasant working experience wherever possible.

1.13 Wool Needles

This is necessary for putting the finishing touches on your work. Purchase a wool needle that has a large eye so that it can easily be threaded with thicker yarn. Additionally, check that the end of the needle is blunt; a pointed needle will split your yarn, which will ruin your work.

1.14 Stitch Makers

These are necessary for both identifying the beginning of your rounds and maintaining your operating loop in place while you work on filling your piece with toy stuffing. You can use open stitch indicators that can be removed or added at any moment, or you can purchase locking stitch markers that close like a sewing needle and will not fall out of your work. Either option is available for purchase. Plastic or metal are the most common materials used to make stitch markers.

1.15 Anti-corrosion pins

When putting together projects, pins are essential for keeping items in place, and blocking your work need pins as well.

1.16 Project bag

A wonderful location in which to store all of the work that is still in progress while ensuring that it is kept clean.

1.17 Notebook and pen

It is helpful for keeping track of any modifications or alterations that you make to a crochet design as you work on it, as well as for adding notes as you crochet.

1.18 The needle and thread for sewing

Essential for attaching felt pieces to your craft and sewing extremely little items together. Also useful for sewing on buttons.

1.19 Protective goggles and facemasks

Used for giving characters a more lifelike appearance and for designing adorable expressions on their faces. They come in sizes ranging from 6 millimeters up to 0.2 inches in increments (15mm). The eye or nose form, which is often made of plastic and includes a shank, and the plastic washer, which is designed to fit over the shank, are the two components that make up safety eyes and noses. Always make sure that you fit your safety eyes and noses according to the instructions provided by the manufacturer, and always perform a safety check after you have fixed your eyes and noses by attempting to take them out to confirm that they are correctly and securely fastened. When it comes to youngsters younger than three years old, the majority of manufacturers do not advise employing safety eyes and laces.

1.20 Spray on Some Starch.

This is an ironing aid, but it can also be used as a stiffener if it is sprayed onto a piece of crochet and then worked from left to right. It works wonderfully for reinforcing delicate goods like the crown of the princess (see page 25). It has a high price tag and may be found in the laundry aisle of most retail establishments.

1.21 Stuffing for Toys

It is advised that children's toys be stuffed with safety toy filler. It will be made very obvious on the bag whether or not the stuffing is safe, hygienic, and washable. You can also choose organic or eco-friendly solutions, which are compostable and less detrimental to the environment. Polyester is now the most commonly used synthetic choice because it is inexpensive, but you can also buy other possibilities.

1.22 Felt and Fabric Pieces

It comes in handy when decorating a project with accessories and putting the finishing touches on it. The higher the percentage of wool in your felt, the higher the quality and hardness, which makes it simpler to embroider and less prone to shred. Wool is a natural fiber that may be obtained from sheep.

Chapter 2:
How To Choose The Appropriate Yarn

When it comes to crochet, one of the most crucial decisions you will have to make is the yarn to use for each of your projects. Essential to one's success is the ability to select the appropriate yarn for their project. In this chapter, we will discuss the many types of fibers that are used in the production of yarn, as well as the weights and gauges of yarn, and how to read a yarn label.

2.1 Yarn Fibers

Yarn can be spun from a variety of materials, but the three most common are animal hair, plant fiber, and synthetic fiber.

- o The following are examples of animal fibers: wool, alpaca, angora, cashmere, and silk.
- o Included in the category of plant fibers are soy, cotton, hemp, bamboo, and linen.
- o Acrylic, polyester, microfibers, and even metallic threads are all examples of synthetic yarn fibers.

The health advantages of different types of fiber are not interchangeable. Acrylic yarn is known for its user-friendliness and low maintenance requirements. Wool is another material that is quite simple to work with, but it does require blocking both after the project is finished and after it is washed. Cotton's ability to absorb water and wick away moisture makes it an excellent material for use in home improvement tasks, including the bathroom and kitchen.

2.2 Yarn Weight

Yarn Weight Chart			
Weight	Description	Recommended Hook	Stitches in 4"
0 Lace	Fingerling, Size 10 Crochet Thread	Steel 1.6-1.4mm/B-1	32-48
1 Superfine	Sock, Fingerling	2.25-3mm/B-1 to E-4	21-32
2 Fine	Sport, Baby	3.4-4.5mm/E-4 to 7	16-20
3 Light	DK, Light Worsted	4.5-5.5mm/7 to I/9	12-17
4 Medium	Worsted, Afghan, Aran	5.5-6.5mm/I-9 to K-10 ½	11-14
5 Bulky	Chunky, Craft, Rug	6.5-9mm/K-10 ½ to M-13	8-11
6 Super Bulky	Super Bulky, Roving	9-15mm/m-13 to Q	7-9
7 Jumbo	Jumbo, Roving	15mm and up	6 or less

There is a weight range for yarn that goes from 0 all the way up to 7. Even weight class 8, which is a giant jumbo yarn used for carpeting and many other crafts related to home decor, could be among the things you find. As the table makes clear, there is a prescribed hook size that corresponds to each weight category. When you go to buy the yarn, you should never buy it without first checking the pattern to determine what grade of yarn is required.

2.3 Gauge

The term "gauge" is used to describe the relationship between the number of stitches across a row in four inches and the number of rows necessary to generate a length of four inches. Always ensure that you have enough time to prepare a gauge swatch before beginning a project. Create a crochet swatch measuring four inches in width by utilizing the specified yarn and hook size from the pattern. First, you will need to count the number of stitches across the row, as well as the number of rows that equal four inches. Then, you will need to compare these figures to the gauge that is specified in the pattern. If your swatch is either too big or too small, you will probably need to switch to a larger or smaller hook size.

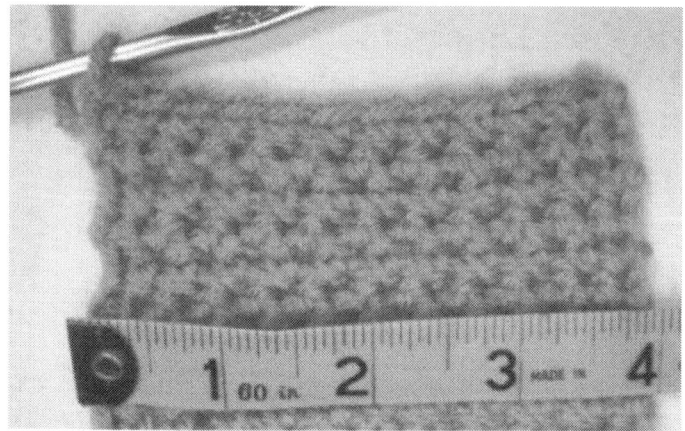

13 stitches across 4 inches

15 rows are equal to 4 inches. In the preceding pictures, I worked with a yarn of medium weight and a hook size I/9, respectively. This resulted in a gauge for me of 13 stitches over a length of four inches and 15 rows for a length of four inches. If you consult the chart that categorizes yarn weights, you will notice that these figures correspond to the gauge that is specified for a yarn of medium weight.

2.4 The Yarn Label

The label on the yarn will provide you with practically all of the information you require concerning that specific yarn. You can discover information about the yarn's fiber volume fraction, thickness, appropriate hook size, gauge when using that hook dimensions, color, and care instructions for laundering on the label of the yarn. The majority of yarn manufacturers implement a better understandings of care symbols on their products. On the website of Lion Brand, you can discover a comprehensive collection of all of these symbols.

We can tell that this particular skein of Red Heart Super Saver yarn is made of acrylic and belongs to the weight category known as four. The hook size advised by the manufacturer is I/9, which ought to provide us with a gauge of 12 solitary crochet stitches across four inches and 15 rows throughout the length of four inches. The finished crocheted fabric can be machine cleaned and dried at temperatures not exceeding 104 degrees Fahrenheit, but it should not be ironed. This yarn does not come with a specific dye lot; however, if it did, you would probably want to buy at least one additional skein of the same dye lot so that you could be certain that the color will be uniform throughout your project.

2.5 Different Yarn For Crochet and Their Use

Which Different Varieties of Yarn Fibers Are There?

The majority of fibers can be classified as either natural or synthetic, depending on their origin.

- **Natural Fibers**

Cotton and bamboo are examples of natural fibers that come from plants, whereas wool and alpaca are examples of natural fibers that come from animals. Silk yarn is still another type of natural fiber yarn, however rather than coming from plants, it is derived from the silkworm. Care instructions for yarn that is often significantly more detailed when it is derived from the animal fiber.

- **The Use of Synthetic Fibers**

Plastics of varying types are woven together to form what is known as synthetic fibers. Acrylic is one of the most prevalent types of plastic. However, these materials can also be made of polyester, rayon, or nylon. Care for synthetic yarns is simple and does not need much effort, as there is no need to worry about washing or drying them after use.

There is also a type of yarn called blended yarn, which is a combination of natural and man-made fibers. Acrylic and cotton blended yarn are one of the blended yarns that may be found most frequently. It depends on the brand and producer of the yarn as to how much of each component there is, but the ratio can be anything from 90/10 acrylic to cotton or cotton to acrylic.

The heaviness of the yarn can be approximated by using the yarn's thickness as a guide. You may evaluate how and when you need to use these varieties of yarn by consulting the chart below, which compares the weight of various yarns.

The CYC Standard weighing Scheme forms the basis for the yarn weights that are explained further down.

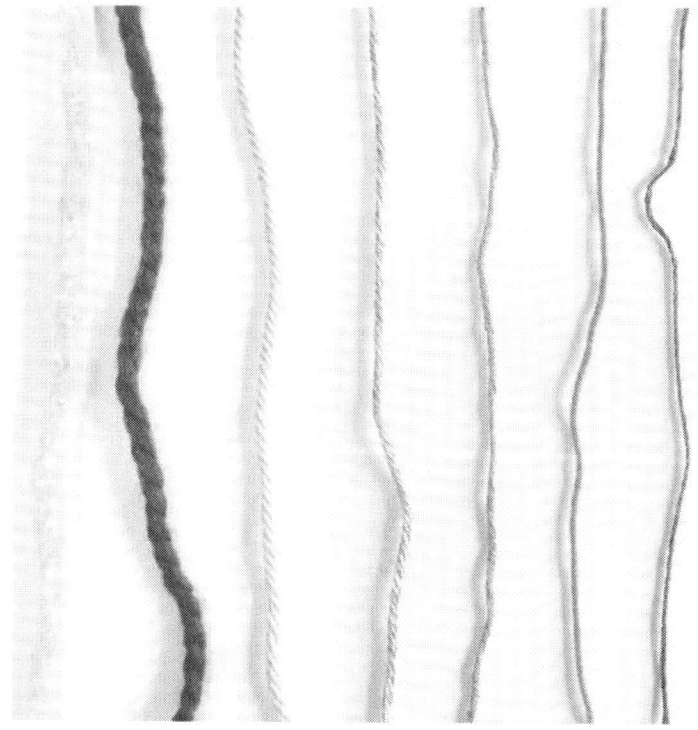

- **Lace or Weight #0 Thread**

Lace yarn, also known as weight #0 yarn, has a fingering or 10-count crochet thread. When working with yarn of this weight, a US hook number of 6/7/8 (stainless steel) and B-1 (regular) is recommended for crocheting. The metric equivalent for steel is 1.6-1.4 millimeters, whereas the standard size for a metric hook is 2.25 millimeters.

Weight #1 or Super Coarse

The sock, fingering, and baby yarn varieties are all included in the weight #1 or "Super Fine" category when crocheting with yarn of this weight. The hook sizes that are frequently used range from B-1 to E-4 in the US and 2.25 to 3.5 mm in the metric system.

- **Weight No. 2 or Very Fine**

The sport and baby yarn varieties are included in the fine or weight #2 category. When crocheting with yarn of this weight, the hook sizes that are frequently used range from E-4 to 7 in the US and 3.5 to 4.5 millimeters in metric.

- **Yarn of Weight #3 or Very Light**

Weight, either 3 or DK and light Worsted are both types of yarn that fall under the category of "light yarn." When crocheting with yarn of this weight, one typically uses hook sizes ranging from 7 to I-9 in the US system and 4.5 to 5.5 mm in the metric system.

- **Yarn of either weight #4 or medium**

The Worsted, Afghan, and Aran varieties of yarn all fall under the category of "weight #4" or "medium" yarn. When crocheting with yarn of a Worsted weight, the hook sizes typically used range from I-9 to K-10 1/2 in the US and 5.5 to 6.5 mm in the metric system.

- **Yarn of weight #5 or the Bulky kind**

Yarn of weight #5, sometimes known as bulky yarn, encompasses the chunky, craft, and rug varieties of yarn. When crocheting with yarn of this weight, one often uses hook sizes ranging from K-10.5 to M-13 in the US standard system and 6.5 to 9 mm in the metric system.

- **Weight #6 or particularly hefty**

The yarn varieties known as super bulky and roving are both included in the weight #6 category, often known as super bulky. When crocheting with yarn of this weight, the hook sizes that are typically used range from M-13 to Q in the US and 9 to 15 mm in the metric system.

- **Jumbo or a weight of #7**

Weight #7, sometimes known as Jumbo, encompasses both the jumbo and roving varieties of yarn. When working with yarn of this weight, the hook sizes Q and bigger in the US and 15 mm and larger in metric are typically recommended for crocheting.

2.6 Types of Yarn

Find out below even more information about each type of fiber that is used to manufacture yarn.

Animal Yarn

Wool, alpaca, silk, cashmere, mohair, and angora are some examples of animal fibers that can be used to make yarn. They have some degree of elasticity and excellent breathability, which enables them to retain air and maintain warmth. Wool, which can technically refer to any fiber shorn from an animal, is the most common type of fiber. Knitters and crocheters, on the other hand, frequently consider wool to originate from the fleece of various breeds of sheep. In the same way that human hair can be coarse or fine, wavy or straight, wool can also be. It can differ from one species of animal to another, or even from one individual animal to another, depending on factors such as age, location, and the part of the animal's body where the wool grew. It retains heat, provides insulation, is breathable, and has a high absorption capacity. In point of fact, wool is capable of absorbing up to thirty percent of its own weight without appearing or feeling wet.

Plant Yarn

Cotton, linen, and bamboo are all examples of plant fibers. Cellulose is the primary component of plant fibers. Cellulose, which is present in all plant species, is responsible for the uptake of water at the plant's roots and its subsequent movement to the plant's leaves and flowers. When people dress in plant fibers, the cellulose in the plant fibers draw moisture away from the body, allowing the moisture to eventually evaporate. Because of this, heat is drawn away from the body. It is commonly believed that plant fibers "breathe nicely," making them ideal for use in summer clothing. They are not elastic; thus, they won't be able to keep their shape very well. They are also heavier, which can result in a garment that is more burdensome to wear. When working with plant fibers, it is essential to pay close attention to the gauge of your work and to carefully organize your project, making sure to take into account the qualities and advantages of the fiber.

Synthetic Yarns

Acrylic, rayon, nylon, and polyester are some examples of that types. They can be washed and dried quickly in the washing machine, making them an excellent choice for items that need to be washed frequently. In addition to these benefits, synthetic fibers are economical, long-lasting, and can be obtained in a plethora of colors. Acrylic is manufactured from ethylene, which is a byproduct of the oil industry. It is pliable and warm, but it does not retain its shape or warmth as well as natural fibers do. It will lead to pilling (the process for when small, firm balls of lint form on the surface of fabrics like clothing) and won't be able to keep its shape very well, but it can withstand multiple washing items.

2.7 Merino Wool

Merino wool, which comes from merino sheep, is one of the most luxurious and soft types of wool. It works wonderfully for any item that will be worn against the skin, such as hats, scarves, mittens, and sweaters, because it is so soft and comfortable.

Lion Brand's LB Collection Super wash Merino Thread and Knit Picks' Swish Worsted are two examples of popular merino yarns.

Because Merino wool yarn is easy to wash and can readily handle be being washed in a machine, it is an excellent choice for clothing that is worn on a daily basis.

2.8 Wool

The hair of sheep is used to make yarn made of wool. During use, wool maintains its warmth while also proving to be resilient. It works particularly well for knitting sweaters, caps, scarves, and gloves. After being washed, several types of wool become smoother and less irritating than when they were first purchased. Additionally, yarns are very fashionable, combining wool and acrylic. It has the suppleness of wool while maintaining the ease of care that acrylics are known for.

Knit Picks' Wool of the Andes and Lion Brand's Fisherman's Wool are two examples of the wool yarns that are particularly well-liked.

Wool is typically more expensive, and the best place to find wool of a high quality is in a shop that specializes in yarn. However, it is possible to find wool in chain stores on occasion. It is possible for wool to have a coarser texture, as in the case of the wool that comes from merino sheep. The percentage of lanolin, which is an essential oil found in wool that is present in organic wool, will be rather high. Wool can be made more water-resistant by adding lanolin.

Naturally occurring, microscopic scales can be found on wool fibers. These scales adhere to one another, and when the wool is washed in hot water and agitated, it felts and becomes more compact as a result. Sometimes knitters and crocheters will build an exceptionally large project with the intention of felting it in order to produce a dense and particularly toasty garment (think mittens). On the other hand, accidents can occur in the washing machine that causes wool creations to feel and shrink. When your beloved sweater shrinks to the point where it can no longer be worn, it's a sad day. Some wool yarns are processed with an acid-based bath or treated with a polymer to prevent this from happening. This either eliminates the scales or prohibits them from binding together, depending on which method is used. The wool gets "super cleaned" as a result of this process, which makes it easier to wash in a machine. On the other hand, this results in a fiber that is severely treated. Hand washing with either hot or cool water and air drying a ball of high-quality wool that has not been super-washed is an effective way to prevent the wool from felting.

2.9 Alpaca Yarn

The hair of an alpaca is used to make yarn out of alpaca fiber. Because of its coziness and its exquisite appearance, this fiber is ideal for use in the construction of anything that will come into direct contact with the skin. In addition to being one of the warmest fibers that can be obtained, it easily combines with a variety of other fibers.

Simply Alpaca, which is sold by Knit Picks, and Sugar Bush Nanaimo Yarn Alpaca Blend are two examples of some of the most well-known alpaca yarns. The fiber from an alpaca is superior than wool in both warmth and softness. In addition to that, it is a little bit fuzzier, and it stretches more easily. The angora goat is the source of the material known as mohair, which is prized for its extreme luster and gloss. It is possible to manufacture a fabric that is light but warm, which is perfect for scarves and garments are worn inside. The Kashmir goat is responsible for producing cashmere. It is far more breathable than wool yet is much lighter overall. It is interesting to note that the goat has two different types of coats: a coarse outer coat that can't be made into thread and a fluffy undercoat that may be turned into cashmere. The fact that each animal only generates a few ounces each year contributes to the high cost of the product.

2.10 Angora Yarn

The coats of Angora rabbits are where the distinctive sort of wool known as angora comes from. Although the systematic abuse of angora rabbits has brought criticism to this beautiful fiber in recent years, it is perfectly possible to create angora wool in a way that is both ethical and sustainable and does not involve the use of any methods that involve the torture of animals.

The average diameter of Angora wool fibers is between 12 and 16 microns, making it one of the tiniest varieties of wool fibers in the world. As a result, Angora wool is exceptionally smooth and plush. This variety of wool is incredibly fluffy, and because the cores of the Angora rabbit hairs are empty, Angora wool has superior properties when it comes to retaining heat compared to the majority of wool varieties. Because it lacks the allergenic qualities that are inherent to other forms of wool, Angora wool is a crucial alternative for individuals who are allergic to the hair of animals.

The most common application for angora wool is in the production of clothing. This sort of wool gained widespread attention as a sweater material, but today it is also utilized to make outerwear such as suit jackets, scarves, and gloves. On occasion, Angora wool is also used to manufacture little throw blankets and covers for pillows. This practice is much less common. In addition, angora wool is a very common craft material that is utilized for knitting.

2.11 Cashmere Yarn

Cashmere and yarns blended with cashmere are two excellent choices for a crocheter's material. They offer a wide variety of possibilities for the final products, and they are easy to manipulate due to their smoothness and gentleness. If they decide to spend a little additional money on yarns and crochet with cashmere, they will be able to make you a genuinely luxurious clothing. This will be their reward to you. For the best results when crocheting with pure quality cashmere yarn, it's important to use a hook and pattern that are up to the task. This will ensure that you get the most out of your cashmere yarn.

To begin, select a hook that is appropriate for the yarn you will be using. Cashmere yarns are available in a wide range of weights; however, the majority of cashmere yarns are either Worsted or Aran weight. Check the label of the yarn for a recommendation on the hook size to use, and then crochet a gauge swatch or two to choose a hook that gives you the size and drape of stitches that you want.

When crocheting with cashmere yarns, you should look for a pattern that corresponds to the yardage you have available. Due to the high cost of cashmere yarn, it is more likely than not that you will only have one or two skeins of it on hand at any given moment. You have an area of less than or equal to around 200 yards to deal with. If you know where to search, you can find a wide selection of crochet patterns that only use one skein of yarn or a tiny amount of it.

After you have finished crocheting your item using your premium yarn, such as cashmere yarn by Consignee, be sure to block it so that it retains its shape. Simply soaking the yarn in water that has wool wash or a mild detergent added to it, then gently squeezing it dry, and laying it flat, is all that is required to block your finished item so that it maintains the desired size and shape.

After you've finished your work, you should wash the finished item. Because cashmere was used in the end product that you crocheted, you will need to exercise additional caution when cleaning it. Wash wool by hand with a light detergent soap or using wool wash, and It should be pinned to a blocking board, an ironing board, or another soft surface, and then it should be allowed to dry flat while being re-blocked as necessary. After that, you can remove the pins, and they will maintain their form without them.

2.12 Silk Yarn

There is a good chance that you have come across yarns and items crafted from silk at some point during your exploration of knitting, crochet, or any of the other fiber arts. You may also be familiar with wearing silk clothing, such as scarves, dresses, shirts, and so on. We are aware that silk has a supple and delicate texture. It comes with very detailed instructions on how to care for it. In addition to that, putting your hands on it can be a little bit scary! Now, what exactly is it? Where does it originate, exactly? The question is, why should we worry?

Silk is a natural textile, just like its bulkier counterpart, wool, which is also a natural fabric. The production of genuine silk does not include the use of any chemicals or the weaving of wool from animals. Insects, on the other hand, are the ones responsible for its creation. Cocoons, which are used to extract silk proteins, are spun by a variety of insects, including caterpillars, worms, and even several species of cricket. The majority of the silk that is sold in stores and online comes from the caterpillars of moths that feed on silkworms. The exquisite cocoons that these caterpillars build out of silk fiber are reminiscent of the webs that spiders spin out of their own "silk." These caterpillars, which are also referred to as silkworms, are bred by commercial silk manufacturers in order to generate white silk thread. When the chrysalises are retrieved, they unwind into a single lengthy thread. This ensures that virtually all the thread may be used and woven into sturdy fabric.

It's possible that you'll notice a slight (or even significant!) difference in the way that working with silk yarn feels like having to work with wool or cotton fabric when you first start knitting or crocheting with silk yarn. It has the potential to feel "slippery" and overly delicate, but it is precisely those qualities that will allow you to create a wonderful, completed product! Not only is a shawl or scarf made of silk delicate and pleasantly warm, but it is also remarkably resilient and long-lasting.

You can begin with the Silk Cocoons themselves if you are feeling up to the enjoyable challenge of doing so. These are available in their original white color as well as in a variety of vibrant pre-dyed hues. Make paper with them, feel with them, make jewelry with them, or even use them for beauty! You may use the silk cocoon to scrub your skin by first soaking it in water that is lukewarm for about three minutes, then placing it on the tip of your finger and rubbing it in circular motions. You might also use them to spin your own yarn with your hands.

When it refers to knitting or crocheting utilizing silk thread, there is a never-ending selection of possibilities from which to choose. Hand Beaded Silk Yarn is one of our favorites since it is really dainty, beautifully colored, and crammed full of teeny-tiny pearls all at the same time. Using beaded yarn transforms your creations from mundane to one-of-a-kind and captivating works of art. A silk yarn of this type can be utilized to construct beautiful shawls, other types of home decorations, and even wall hangings in the bohemian style. It is not difficult to become addicted to working with silk yarn, despite the fact that knitting or crocheting with it will appear a little strange at first.

2.13 Silky Soy Yarn

A yarn could potentially be spun from soy fiber, although this is quite unlikely. It has the brilliance of silk but the strength of steel, and it is both soft and tough. In addition to this, soy fiber retains its color well and drapes beautifully. It is a choice that is 100% natural and beneficial to your health, since it possesses antibacterial qualities and amino acids that improve the condition of your skin.

In the 1930s, Henry Ford developed car-seat upholstery using a mixture of soybean and sheep's wool for the first time. This was the first-time soy was used in the textile industry. The byproducts of the industries that produce tofu and soy-based foods are where the soy yarn fiber derives from. Okara is the name given to the liquid form of the usable residues after soybean processing. Okara is processed by a step known as "wet-spinning," which results in the removal of soy proteins, which are then dried. After the proteins have been dried, yarn is made from them using the defatted soy protein individually or in combination with other fibers like wool or cotton. The operation is kind to the environment and generates very little, if any, trash.

Because soy can be blended with such a wide variety of fibers, yarns made from soy and soy blends can look and behave very differently from one another. The following analysis compares five different yarns that differ in appearance, texture, and weight.

The use of soy in the production of yarn is a more recent development. It has a gorgeous shine and drape, and it is frequently combined with wool or acrylic because of these qualities.

2.14 Cotton Yarn

As we go into the warmer sections of the year here in the Northern Hemisphere, a yarn made of cotton is the most suitable option for crocheting. Cotton fiber results in products that are not only breathable but also exceptionally robust and long-lasting. Cotton tends to produce a yarn that is on the heavier side, particularly once it has become wet. When considering projects, give special consideration to the amount of yarn that will be required. Naturally, cotton thread and cotton of sock weight will have a lower density in comparison to the cotton of Worsted weight or bulky weight. Unless, of course, you're working on a particularly thick product that you intend to be somewhat weighty. Cotton, as a general rule, does not stretch. Because of this, it is an excellent material for things that are supposed to be strong and long-lasting. Because of this property, cotton yarn is an excellent choice for crocheting amigurumi, market tote bags, dish towels, and crochet baskets. Lion Brand Kitchen Towels and potholders are commonly crafted out of items like cotton yarn, which is an example of a yarn made entirely of cotton. Cotton that has been mercerized has been handled in a way that makes it appear to have a higher sheen. The disadvantage is that it often has a lower absorption capacity than cotton that has not been mercerized. When it comes to crochet, either one can be an excellent choice; nonetheless, you will need to make your decision carefully based on the qualities you want the ultimate product to have. If you wish to color your own cotton yarn, this is another important consideration you'll need to give careful attention to. "If the yarn is not pendants illuminating (a method that straightens the fiber, makes it less likely to decrease when washed, and makes the yarn have a glossy finish, flashier finish), each loop in a stitch is sealed into place from the contact pressure of the other loops in the stitch," explains crochet designer Emjay Bailey of Nerdigurumi. "If the yarn is mercerized, however, each loop in a stitch is free to move freely." Because the strands do not slip, slide, or shift, this indicates that the integrity and structure of the threads and rows keep out well, and that finished ends that have been woven in are virtually locked in.

Cotton yarn is made entirely of cotton and is an excellent material for creating durable items such as washcloths, dishcloths, and everything else that needs to stand the test of time.

Lace crafts and filet crochet techniques almost always call for the utilization of cotton thread fiber. It is an ultrafine yarn with a weight of 1 that is available for a low price at the majority of craft businesses located locally.

2.15 Hemp Yarn

This is one of the yarns that is the least harmful to the environment. The plant that is used to make it grows far more quickly than cotton does and generates a significantly greater quantity of fiber. Although it was traditionally used for weaving and macramé, crocheting and knitting with it are becoming increasingly popular as an alternative application for the yarn. It is not only durable but also rather comfortable and soft to the touch. Hand washing is required for hemp. Before beginning to knit, knitters should be aware of the many benefits and drawbacks associated with working with hemp yarn. It is an excellent yarn for use in the creation of placemats and market bags, and it also produces excellent dishcloths when combined with cotton and perhaps other absorbing plant fibers. But there are circumstances in which you should steer clear of hemp.

Hemp yarn does offer a few distinct benefits that set it apart from other options and make it a desirable option for certain knitting tasks. The following is a list of some of the specific advantages that using hemp yarns in your knitting projects can bring:

- o Sturdy & durable
- o Excellent insulator
- o Absorbent
- o Resistant to mildew and mold
- o Non-pilling
- o Gets softer with each wash
- o Absorbs dye well
- o Withstands the effects of fading

The durability of hemp makes it an excellent material for use in products such as shopping bags, tablecloths, and other home goods or personal accessories. It does become more pliable with continued laundering (because of its similarity to linen yarns). In addition, when mixed with cotton, it makes an excellent combination that, when knitted, results in dishcloths that are both robust and absorbent.

2.16 Bamboo Yarn

The texture of these yarns can be described as smooth, light, and soft. It has an air of refined sophistication. It falls elegantly, making it an excellent choice for clothing that requires fluidity. Because it does not retain heat as well as other varieties of yarn, it is ideal for use in summer clothing. The yarn made from bamboo is highly absorbent. The grass of the bamboo plant is turned into a fiber and then spun into bamboo yarn. Because bamboo can be picked without causing the plant's death, the yarn that is produced from it is kind to the environment. The yarn knits up well, resulting in a garment that has an amazing drape. The bamboo plants that are used to make bamboo yarn may be picked without causing any harm to the plant, making it an environmentally benign material. It is manufactured from bamboo grass, which is processed into cellulose, and then the cellulose is spun into a yarn to provide a silky-smooth texture.

Because of its glossy appearance and its low weight, this fiber is ideal for use in projects appropriate for the spring and summer seasons. Because the fibers of bamboo are inherently silky soft, and smooth, the yarn made from bamboo provides for exceptionally soft shawls, cardigans, and other garments. It is frequently combined with other fibers to provide a more varied and textural end product. One of the most well-liked yarns made from bamboo is Lion brand's Truboo Yarn.

2.17 Linen Yarn

The flax plant is used to extract the fiber that is used to make linen. It has been around since the time of the ancient Egyptians. It is a material that is quick to dry, absorbent, breathable, and cool to the touch. The use of linen in the production of lightweight summer clothing or other household accessories is recommended. It can be washed in a machine. The flax plant is the source of linen, which is one of the earliest fibers that have been utilized by humans. It is sturdy and long-lasting, but it is not flexible. Despite this, it does become more comfortable to wear and wash over time. In order to keep the silkiness of the finished product, it is frequently blended with other fibers, such as wool. Before you begin knitting with linen yarn, there are a few things you should be aware of. Linen yarn is a terrific choice for knitting (particularly for light summer tank tops and tees), but there are a few things you should know beforehand. To be sure, it possesses a number of distinct benefits that make linen yarn a delight to work with; on the other hand, it also possesses a number of drawbacks that knitters need to take into consideration, particularly before using linen as a replacement yarn for a knitting project.

When it comes to knitting, linen yarn is one of the best fibers to use. The following is a list of some of the specific advantages that knitting with linen can bring to your projects:

- Strong
- Smooth
- Moisture wicking
- Fast drying
- Non-pilling
- Anti-fungal & antibacterial
- Gets softer with each wash

Because of its ability to dissipate heat and wick away moisture, linen is an excellent choice for the clothing worn in warm climates. It gets softer over time and with repeated washings, which results in the clothing created in linen becoming silky and draping beautifully. It is also an excellent option for use in the production of hand towels and washcloths due to its capabilities of wicking away moisture and inhibiting the growth of bacteria.

2.18 Acrylic Yarn

Acrylic is one of the most popular types of fibers that are used in the production of yarn. Since the acrylic yarn is produced using chemicals such as petroleum, we classify it as a fiber that is derived from fossil fuels. Find out more about the manufacturing process of acrylic fiber, and evaluate whether or not it would be a good option for you.

Another of the most frequent form of yarn is made of acrylic fibers. It is a synthetic, or man-made, material that lends itself well to a wide variety of endeavors and expertise levels. It is manufactured using poly compounds, a type of plastic, that are melted down and shaped into thin strands before being woven together. After that, the process of converting it into yarn is quite similar to the process of turning any other fiber into yarn. First, the filaments are spun together into yarn, and then the yarn is wound into a skein, which you can pick up at your local craft store.

Acrylic yarn is well-known for its strength and durability, and it can be purchased in a dizzying array of colors. If you have been making things with yarn for a while, there is a good chance that you have already chosen an acrylic version of the yarn from the shelves without even recognizing it.

Acrylic yarn is a Cost-Effective Option Acrylic yarn is inexpensive to produce since the synthetic materials that are utilized in its manufacture are readily available and inexpensive. This results in the yarn being more affordable than skeins created from other materials, particularly those based on animal fibers such as wool. Even when considering more expensive, superior acrylic choices, the product must be cost-effective in order to be produced at an affordable price. Acrylic Yarn is Resilient to Wear and Tear. The excellent durability of synthetic fiber over time can be attributed to the thoughtful construction of the material. Because it is such an exceptionally long-lasting material, it is ideal for use in projects with a long-time horizon, such as the construction of sweaters and caps that will be used by people for many years. Even after being washed, there is only a small risk that it may become stretched out and lose its shape. Because it is so simple to manufacture, acrylic fiber is typically quite affordable. You shouldn't have any trouble locating this yarn in any of the local stores. Red Heart Soft and Red Heart Super Saver are two that aren't difficult to track down and are both reasonably priced and easy to find.

Chapter 3:
Crochet Stitches, Abbreviations, and Symbols

In this chapter, we will go over the fundamental crochet stitches that are utilized in designs, as well as the abbreviations and symbols that correspond to those stitches. Textual patterns, charts, graphs, and schematics all make use of these acronyms and symbols in various capacities. If you currently understand how to crochet, then you may use this chapter as a brief review to brush up on your skills. This section will introduce your basic crochet stitches that you can use in any pattern. If you are just starting out, then this is the chapter for you.

3.1 Chain Stitch

Abbreviation: ch

Symbol: ◯ or ◯

Make a knot that will slip, and then lay it on the hook. After doing a yarn over (placing the yarn over the hook), pull the yarn through the slip knot that is located on the hook. A chain stitch is shown here. To crochet the next chain stitch, you will need to yarn over and then draw the yarn through the loop that is located on the hook.

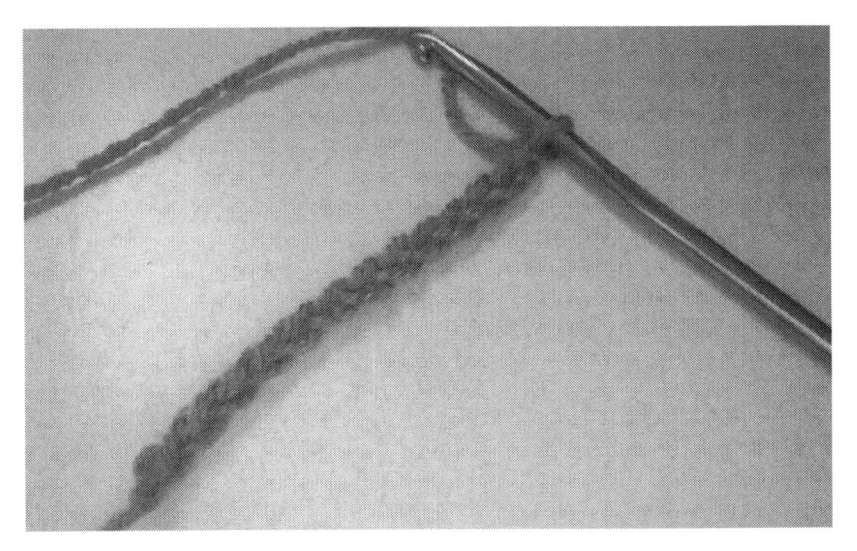

3.2 Slip Stitch

Abbreviation: sl st

Symbol: ●

It is possible to shift the yarn to the correct location in a design by using the slip stitch, which is also used to combine rounds of crochet. To complete this step, put the hook into the subsequent stitch, yarn over, and draw the yarn through both the stitch and the loop that is on the hook.

3.3 Single crochet stitch

Abbreviation: sc

Symbol: ✗

The thick cloth results from using a single crochet stitch. Chain 12. Put the hook into the two chains down from the hook. It is believed to be the initial single crochet stitch in the row when the chain stitch is skipped. To complete the chain stitch, yarn over and pull the working yarn through the chain.

You should see two loops on the hook at this point. Turn the work over and draw the yarn through the two loops simultaneously. This is a single stitch worked in crochet. After yarning over and pulling through the next chain stitch, insert the hook into the next chain stitch, yarn over again, and pull through both loops on the hook.

Continue working your way across the chain by inserting a single crochet stitch into each of the chain stitches that are left. Turn the piece over after you have completed the final stitch.

To start a new row of single crochet, chain 1 at the beginning of the row. This is the initial single crochet stitch of the row, which will be tallied in the total number of stitches you need to make. Instead of inserting the hook into the base of the chain one, you will insert it into the next stitch. Repeat the previous step, yarning over and pulling through the stitch, then yarning over and pulling through the two loops on the hook. Work a single crochet stitch into each stitch until you reach the end of the row. The last stitch is worked into the foundation chain's skipped chain. This completes the pattern. The last stitch of the previous row must be worked into the first chain of the starting chain at the beginning of the following row and every row afterward. Always remember that the initial single crochet should be worked into the stitch immediately after the beginning chain of 1 and not into the base of chain 1.

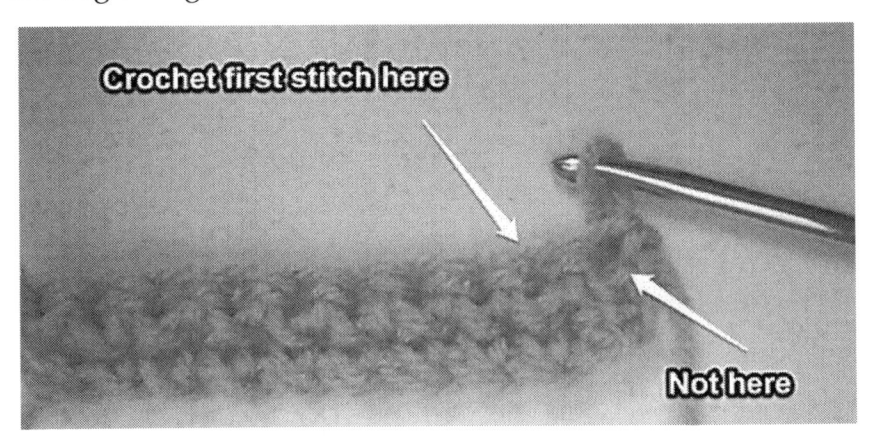

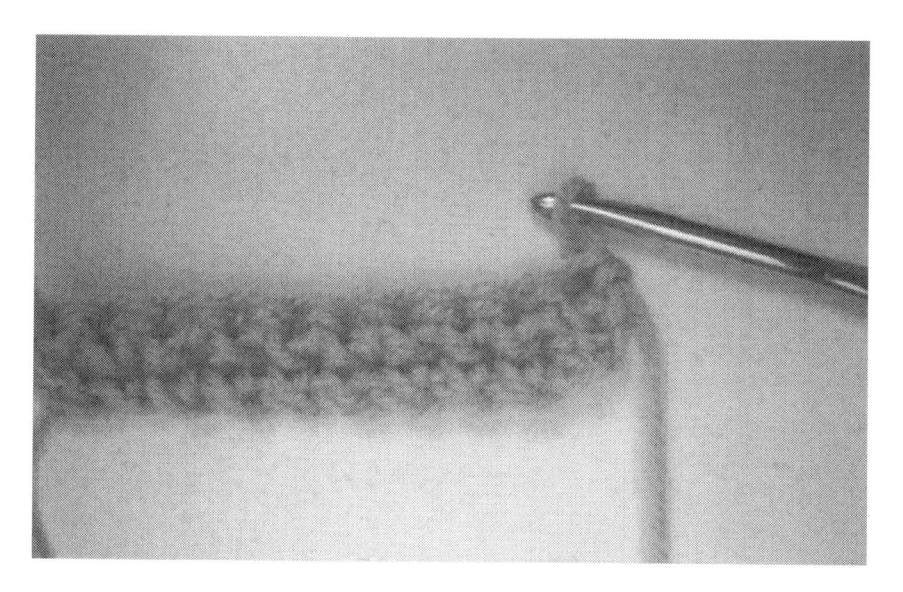

2 Rows of Single Crochet Stitch

3.4 Double Stitch Crochet

The double crochet stitch is the foundation for many other crochet patterns, including the shell stitch, the cluster stitch, and the puff stitch, amongst many others. If you start with a foundation chain, you should skip the first three chains, yarn over, and place the hook into the fourth chain from the hook. The initial double crochet stitch is regarded to be the first three chains that have been skipped. Turn the yarn and draw it through the chain before turning it again. You should see three loops on the hook at this point. Turn your work and pull through the first two loops once you've earned over.

Turn your work and pull through the two loops that are left. This particular stitch is called a double crochet stitch. To start the next stitch, you will need to yarn over and place the hook into the stitch directly in front of you. Turn the work and yarn over twice before pulling through the chain and the first two loops on the hook. Turn the work and yarn over, then draw through the two remaining loops on the hook. Make a chain of 12, and then practice your double crochet by working into each of the chains. When you have concluded, switch over your work.

Make three chains to start the following row. The turning chain is referred to as the three chains because they are thought to be the initial double crochet on the next row. Turn the work and place the hook into the next stitch rather than the beginning of the third chain from the hook. After yarning over and pulling through the stitch, you will need to yarn over and pull through two loops on the hook before moving on to the last two loops. Continue working across the row until you reach the last stitch, at which point you will insert it into the third chain of the starting chain. Every subsequent row should begin with a chain of three, and the very last stitch of the row should be worked into the third chain of the turning chain.

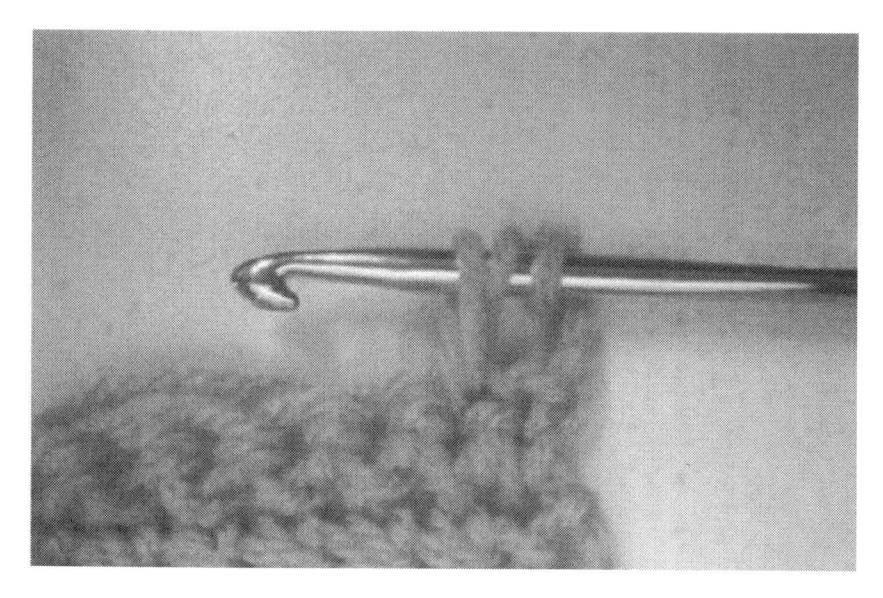

To begin, yarn over and pull through the first stitch. Then, put the hook into the next

stitch and yarn over again

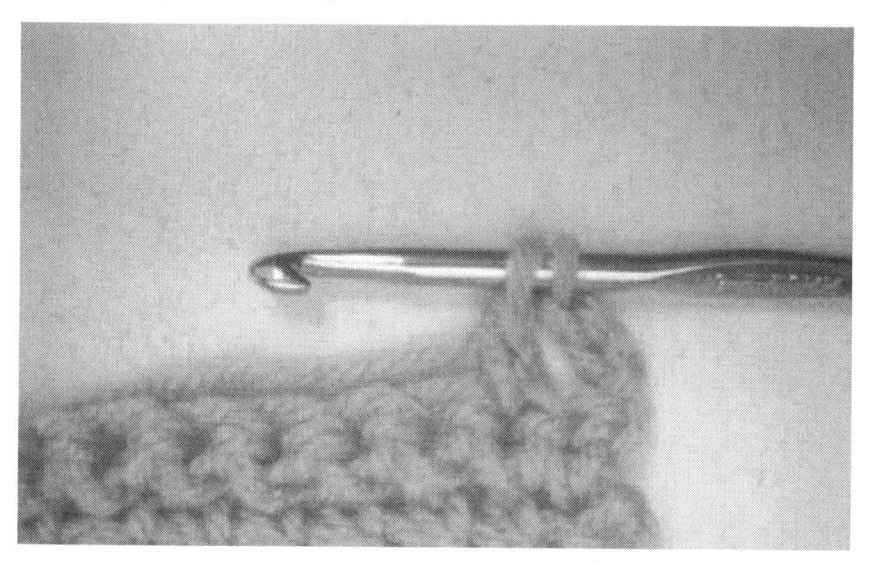

Turn the work and yarn over twice, then pull through the first two loops on the hook.

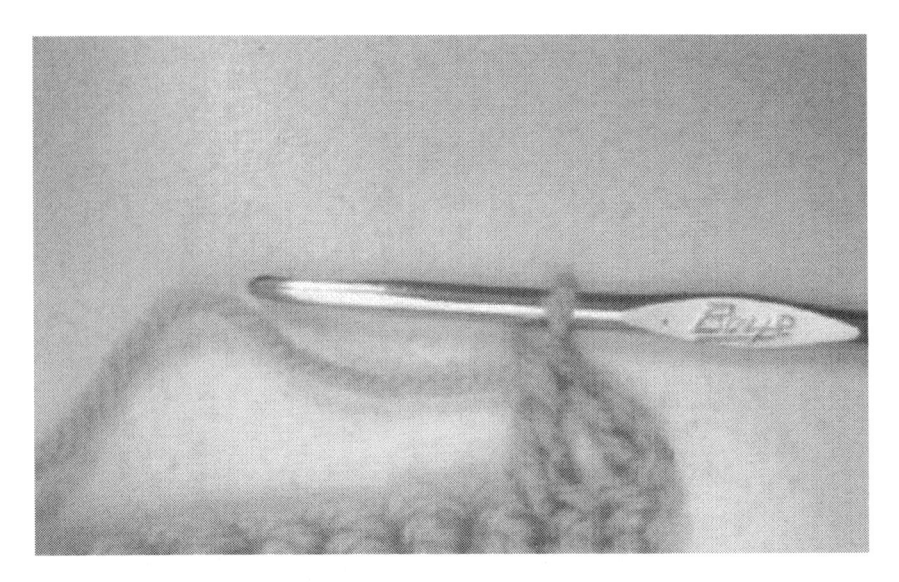

Turn the work with a yarn over and draw through the two remaining loops on the hook.

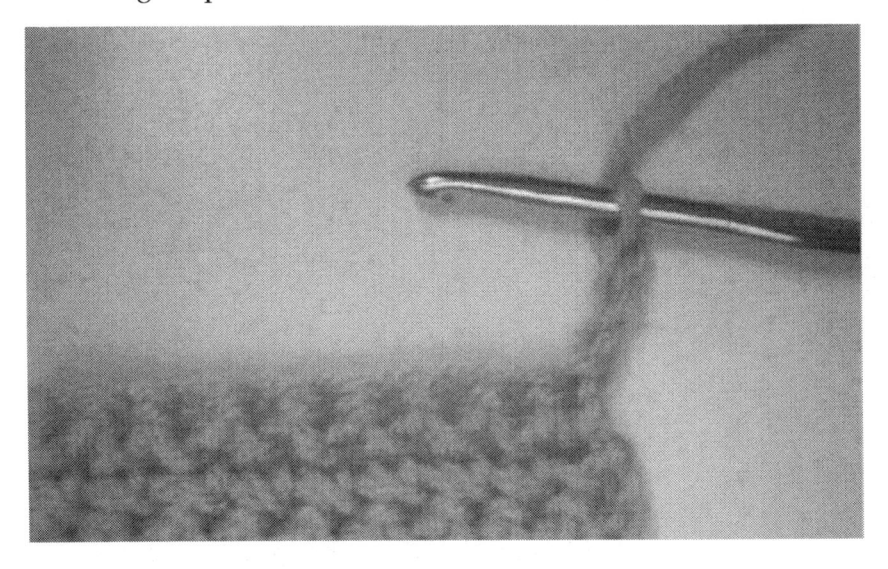

To start a new row, chain 3 stitches.

3.5 The Half Double Crochet Stitch

The single crochet produces a thicker fabric than the half-double crochet, which produces a less dense fabric than the double-crochet. By skipping two chains, yarning over, and inserting the hook into the third chain from the hook, one may begin to make a foundation chain. The initial half double crochet stitch is believed to be these two chains that have been skipped. To complete the chain stitch, yarn over and pull through all links. You should see three loops on the hook at this point. Turn the work over and pull through all three loops using the yarn over technique. The stitch that you see here is called the half-double crochet stitch. Start with a chain of 12 and work some practice half double crochet stitches across the chain. Once you have completed the last stitch, turn in your work. To start a new row of chain 2, begin. This is the beginning of the first half of the double crochet stitch, also referred to as the turning chain. Turn the work with the yarn over and place the hook into the next stitch rather than the beginning of the second chain. Turn the work with the yarn over and draw it through the stitch. Turn the work over and draw the yarn through each of the three loops on the hook. Continue to work across the row, and when you reach the end, work the last stitch into the second chain of the turning chain.

3.6 Treble Crochet Stitch

The treble crochet stitch, often known as the triple crochet stitch, results in a very airy and lax fabric. To begin with a foundation chain, yarn over twice, skip the first five chains, and place the hook into the sixth chain from the hook. This will create the foundation chain. The first stitch is regarded to be the first five chains that have been skipped. To complete the chain stitch, yarn over and pull the working yarn through the chain.

You should see that there are now four loops on the hook. After making a yarn over and pulling it through the first two loops, make another yarn over and draw it through the next two loops, and then make a yarn over and pull it through the last couple of loops on the hook. Start with a chain of 12 and work treble crochet across it. Turn in your work once you have finished the final stitch.

Chain five stitches at the beginning of each new row you work in treble crochet. These are the initial stitch, and they also count as the turning chain. Wrap the yarn around the hook twice before inserting it into the next stitch rather than the beginning of chain five. Turn the work with the yarn over and draw it through the stitch. Three times, yarn over and pull through both loops on the hook to complete this step. When you get to the end of the row, you will work the last stitch into the fifth chain that was skipped, which is also the fifth chain in the beginning.

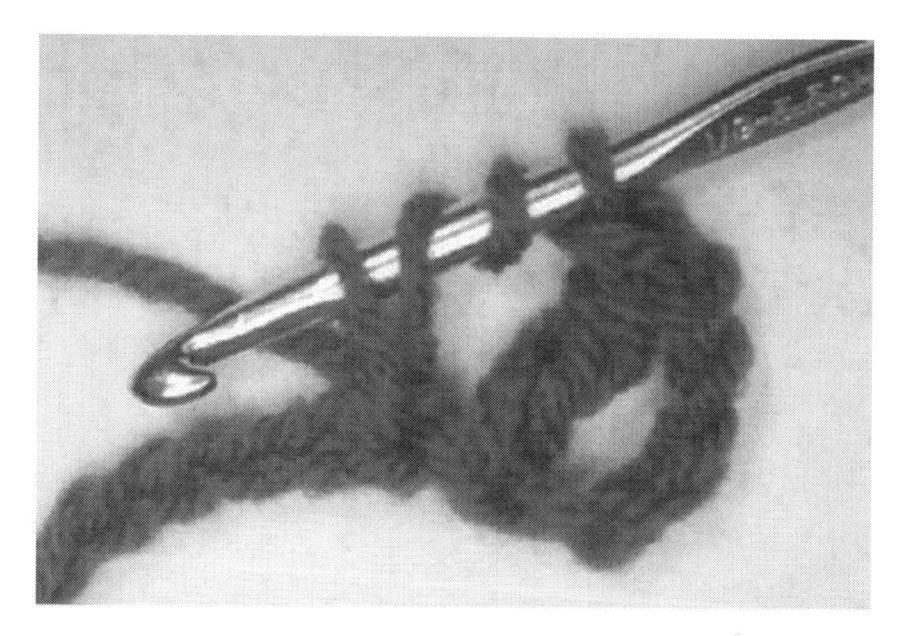

Wrap the yarn around the hook before inserting it into the next stitch. Wrap the yarn around and pull it through.

To finish the stitch, you will need to yarn over three times and pull through the initial two loops on the hook.

3.7 Stitch In The Sand

Utilizing the slip stitch allows the yarn to be moved to the appropriate location in the design. In addition, you may link a foundation chain with this stitch to crochet in the round. After inserting the hook into the correct stitch and doing a yarn over, draw the yarn through both the stitch and the loop on the hook.

The Back Loop Stitch and the Front Loop Stitch

If you examine a crochet stitch closely, you will see that the top loops create a "V" tilted to the side. In most cases, you will position the hook such that it goes under both of these loops. When working back loop or front loop stitches, the hook is only inserted beneath a single loop at a time. For instance, if you see blood written out in a design, you should start double crochet by inserting the hook beneath the back loop of the next stitch and nowhere else. The abbreviation for "front loop double crochet" is "flodc." Ridges are created on both the correct and incorrect sides of the cloth by the back and front loops.

Back Loop Stitch

Front Loop Stitch

3.8 Double Crochet 2 OR 3 Together

dc 2tog or dc3tog Symbol: /|\ or /|\

Dc2tog: means to crochet over and put the hooks into the same stitch twice in quick succession. Do a crochet over and draw through the initial two loops on the hook, then do a crochet over and draw through the remaining two loops. To complete this step, yarn over and put the hook into the following stitch. Next, yarn over and draw through the stitch. Finally, crochet over and draw through the initial two loops on the hook. The hook has been given a total of three loops at this point. To finish the stitch, you will need to crochet over and draw through as many as three loops at the same time.

Dc3tog: Crochet over and put the hook into the following stitch to complete the Dc3tog stitch. Do a crochet over and draw through the initial two loops on the hook, then do a crochet over and draw through the last two loops. To complete this step, yarn over and put the hook into the next stitch. Next, yarn over and draw through the stitch. Finally, crochet over and draw through the initial two loops on the hook. To complete this step, yarn over and insert the hook into the next stitch. Next, yarn over and draw through the stitch. Finally, yarn over and draw through the initial two loops on the hook. The hook has been given a total of four loops at this point. To finish the stitch, you will need to crochet over and draw through as many four loops at the same time.

3,9 Cluster Stitch

Symbol:

After yarning over and inserting the hook into the subsequent stitch, draw the yarn through the stitch before yarning over again. Repeat the previous method using the following four stitches. The hook has been looped a total of seven times at this point. Turn the work over and draw through as many seven loops simultaneously using the yarn-over technique. The stitch is secured by chaining one.

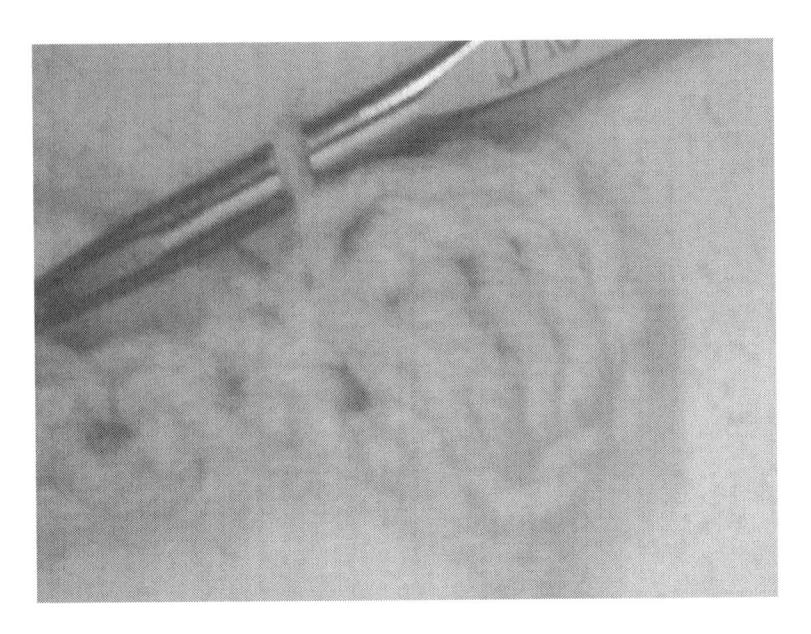

You might also find cluster stitches that have a different number of stitches. Take a look at the symbol to determine the number of stitches that are required to complete the cluster stitch.

3.10 Shell Stitch

Shell st Symbol:

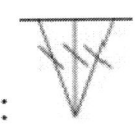

The three double crochet shell stitch is created by working three double crochet stitches into a single stitch. You might also come across shell stitches, which are characterized by the incorporation of five, seven, nine, or more double crochet stitches into a single stitch. Consider looking at the emblem to determine the number of stitches necessary to complete a shell stitch.

3.11 Stitches in the Front and Back of the Post

If you look at a crochet stitch, you will see a post positioned behind the loops that make up the stitch. The stitch is worked around the post while doing a back or front post stitch; it is not worked through the loops of the thread. For instance, the front post double crocheted stitch (fpdc) starts with a yarn over, followed by the insertion of the hook from the front to the back around the post of the following stitch. Wrap the yarn around the post and draw it up to the same height as the other stitches in the row before yarning over again. Proceed with the stitch as you normally would. A front post stitch forms a vertical ridge on the right side of the cloth. A front post stitch will form a vertical ridge on the wrong side of the cloth

To start a back post, double crocheted yarn over and enter the hook from backside to the front around the post of the next stitch. Then, pull the yarn through both loops on the hook. After yarning over, wrap the yarn around the post, pull it up until it is level with the other stitches in the row, and then finish the stitch as you normally would.

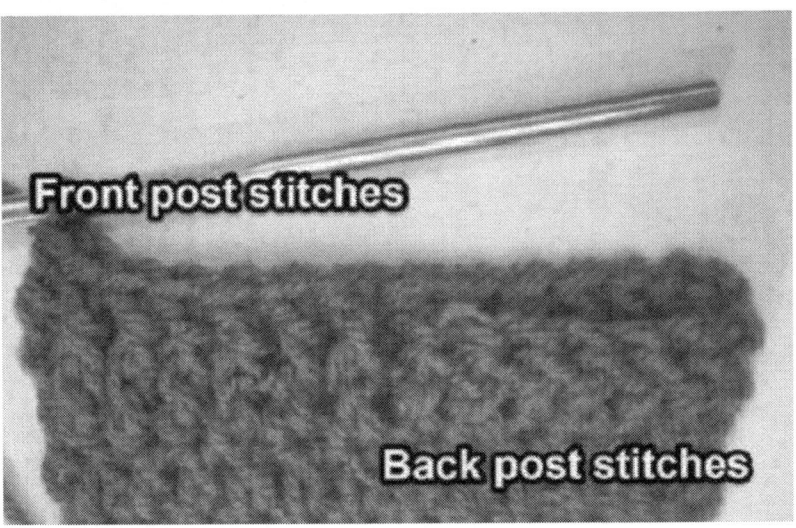

3.12 Increases

When crocheting beanies and hats from the crown down to the brim, you will need to apply increases to give the hat the desired form and bring it to the appropriate size. Crochet more than one stitch into a single stitch is all required for an increase. For instance, if the pattern instructs you to "2dc into the next stitch," you should make two double crochet stitches into the same thread.

Increases may be found in various designs, such as the peaks of a ripple pattern. They can also be used to shape clothes and serve various other functions.

3.13 Decreases

If you are cropping a hat from the brim up to the crown, you will need to reduce the number of stitches to properly form the crown. This is achieved by crocheting two stitches together to create one larger stitch. For instance, if you see sc2tog written in a design, you should combine two single crochet stitches to create one larger stitch. After yarning over and pulling through the first stitch, insert the hook into the stitch. After yarning over and pulling through the next stitch, insert the hook into the next stitch. You should see three loops on the hook at this point. To crochet the two stitches together, you will need to yarn over and pull through all three loops simultaneously.

A dc2tog, or double crochet two together, is created by inserting the hook into the beginning knot, yarning over and pulling through, and then yarning over and pulling through the primary two loops on the hook. The next step is to yarn over, pull through all three loops on the hook, then to yarn over or even pull through the primary two loops. Following a yarn over, the hook should be inserted into the next stitch. Finish the stitch by yarning over and drawing through all three on the hook at once.

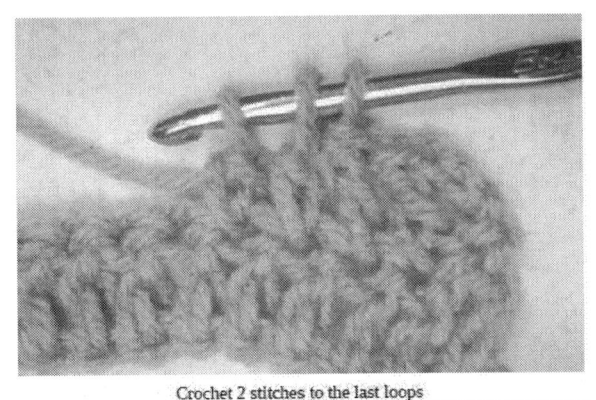

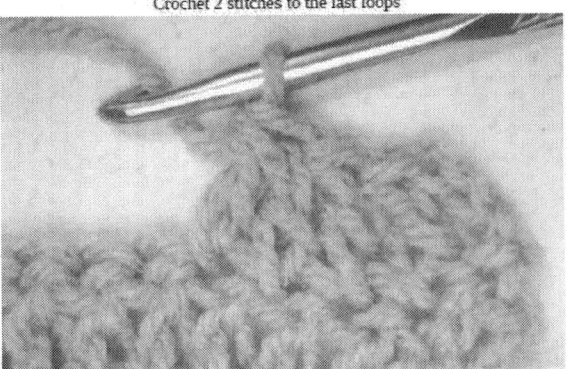

Crochet 2 stitches to the last loops

Dc2tog

3.14 Crochet Stitches Worked Around a Circle

In contrast to crocheting flat, you will need to crochet in the round to create items such as caps, cowls, and motifs. The act of crocheting in rows, both back and forth, is called flat crochet. You crochet around and around while working in rounds, just as the name suggests. Because you never turn your work until instructed by the pattern, the correct side of the cloth will always be facing you while you sew.

To begin, create a chain of 4 (or the number specified in the pattern). Slip stitch when inserting the hook into the initial chain of the project. This creates a ring and links the chain together. After you have completed the first chain of the starting chain, you will normally place the hook into the middle of the ring for the first round of the project. For instance, chain 3, and then double crochet into the loop for the number of stitches provided. If you work with a bigger loop, the design may instruct you to crochet the first round into the chain stitches. Always pay close attention to the points in the design that instruct you to begin crocheting the first round's stitches.

After you have finished one round, complete the circle by doing a slip stitch to connect to the third chain from the beginning (or the top of the starting chain). To keep track of the beginning and end of each round, mark the first stitch of each new round using a stitch marker with a clip attached to it. As each round is completed, you should shift the stitch marker to the first stitch of the next round.

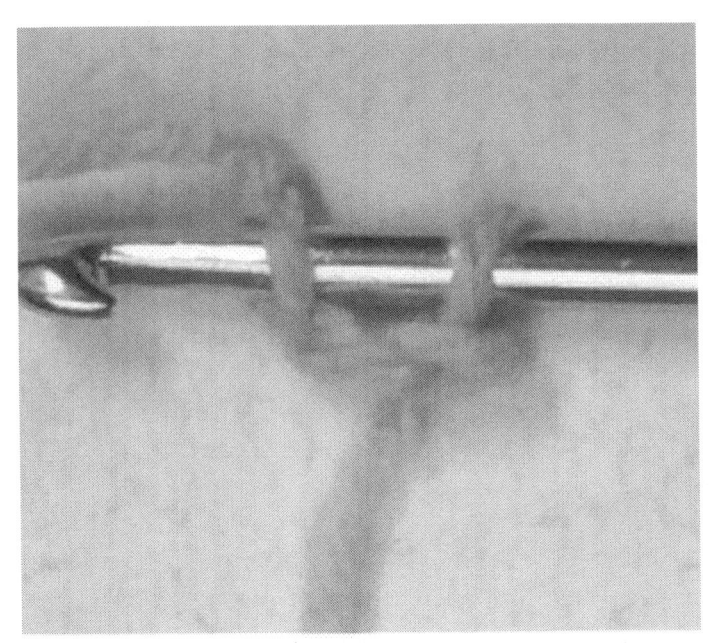

Chain 3 and slip stitch into the first chain to join and form a ring.

3.15 Alterations In Color

Utilizing different hues is one method for communicating your creative side to others. Changing colors as you crochet is a simple process. Continue working in the previous color until the stitch is complete and two loops are on the hook. First, you will need to draw the new color through these two loops, and then you may work the stitches with the new color. My preferred method for incorporating the previous color into the first stitch of the new color is to put the yarn over the new color before beginning the next crochet stitch. This allows me to preserve the previous color.

This preserves the previous color and makes the new color more reliable. Work the final stitch in the row or round until two loops are on the hook.

Changing colors at the end of the row or round is necessary. Take the new color, and thread it through these loops in the chain. Now, crochet the first chain stitch of the new row while positioning the old color so that it is on top of the new color. The previous hue has been preserved. If you want to change the color of the yarn every other row, you should leave the previous color where it is and not cut it, which is also referred to as fastening off. When you get to the end of the row and come back across it, work the final stitch as if you were going to make it until two loops are left on the hook. Then take the previous color and draw it through that stitch. Make the starting chain of the next row with the color you just completed working with. Do this so the color transition is seamless. When you are going to be switching between two different colors, make sure the colors are carried up the side of the cloth. This helps the yarn remain tight and reduces the number of tails that need to be woven in.

~ 78 ~

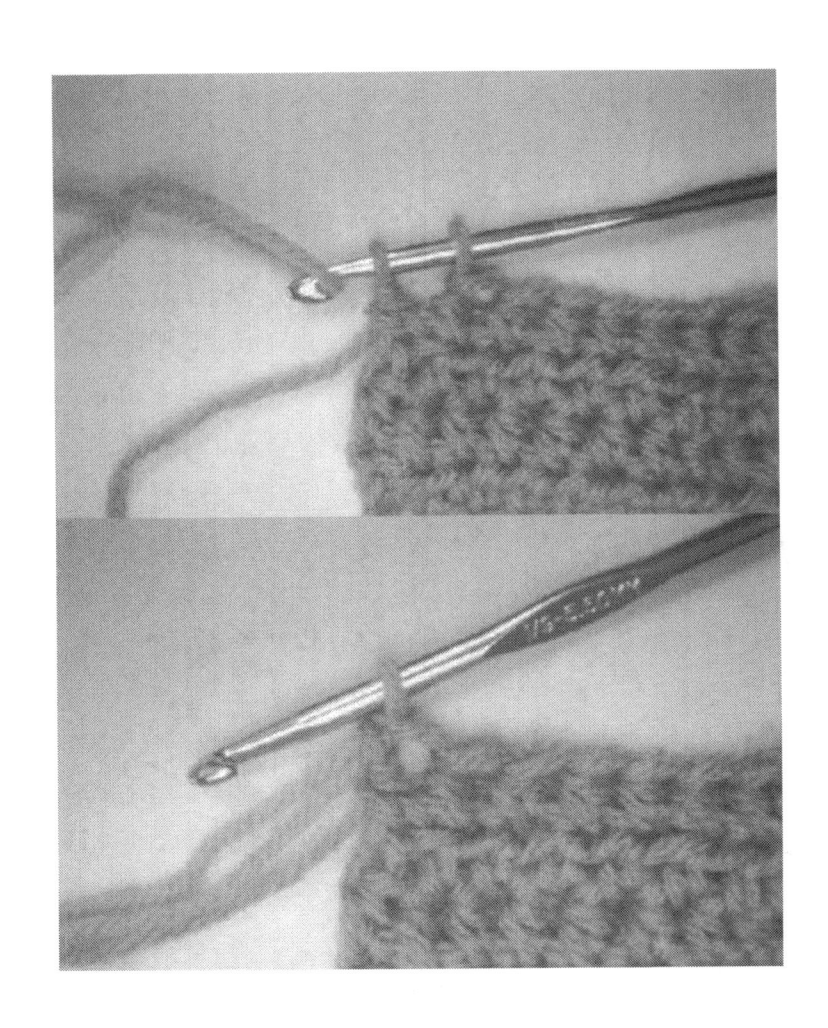

3.16 Techniques For Safely Weaving in Tails

When you finish working with the yarn and cut it or fasten it off, allow at least six inches to weave in. Bring the wrong side of the tails to the front of the cloth. Pass the tail through a needle with a blunt end or a tapestry needle. Weave the tail between the stitches for approximately an inch, going in and out of them. Flip the piece of work over and weave the tail back and forth in and out of the stitches for another inch. One more time, turn the piece of work and weave the tail in and out of the stitches for another inch's worth. The tail is held in place by this, preventing it from wriggling its way out of the work and creating more complications.

3.17 Correct Crochet Hook Grip

When you are just beginning to learn how to crochet, it is easy to fall into the trap of thinking that there is a right way and a wrong way to accomplish things. The excellent thing is that you are free to grip the crochet hook in any way that feels comfortable to you. It would be best if you experimented with both of the standard grips to determine which one best suits your needs. Anyone, regardless of whether they are left- or right-handed, can use one of these approaches. Then, once you've decided how you'll be holding the yarn while crocheting, go ahead and have some fun learning how to do it!

- **Method#1: The Pencil Grip**

Put the tips of both index and thumb fingers together and pinch the flat section of the hook. Keep an eye out for the thumb support, which should be the flat area on the crochet hook. Position the thumb of your dominant hand so that it rests on the thumb rest, then use your index finger to squeeze the opposite direction of the hook.

- When you have a firm grasp on the crochet hook, rotate the base of the hook so that it faces you. With this method, it is possible to determine whether or not the loop of a stitch lands on the throat, which is the terminus of the hook.

Put the hook on the middle finger of your other hand as if it were a pencil. As you would when holding a pencil, bring the remaining of your fingers downwards so that they point towards your palm, and let the hook rest on your middle finger.

- If you place the pencil on the ring finger most of the time, you could attempt to rest your hook there instead. You will probably find that the method that you typically employ provides the greatest level of comfort for you.

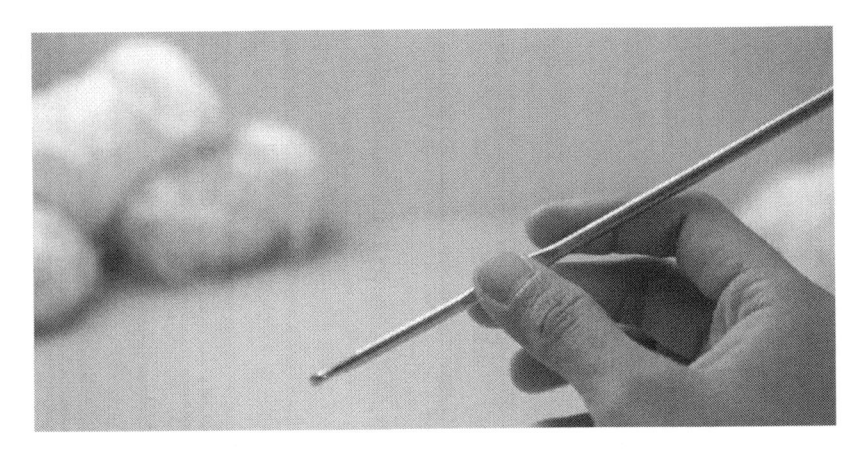

During the crocheting process, you should use your fingers to guide the hook. The pencil grasp is a good strategy to begin with if you want to keep your fingers near to the stitches that you are working on or if you occasionally put the index finger on a strand that you are crocheting. Both of these techniques are common when crocheting. This is due to the fact that the action of crocheting is controlled by your fingers rather than your wrist.

- o If you plan to crochet for an extended amount of time, many individuals believe that the pencil grasp provides the most comfortable experience. This takes place as a result of the length of the hook resting on your hand.

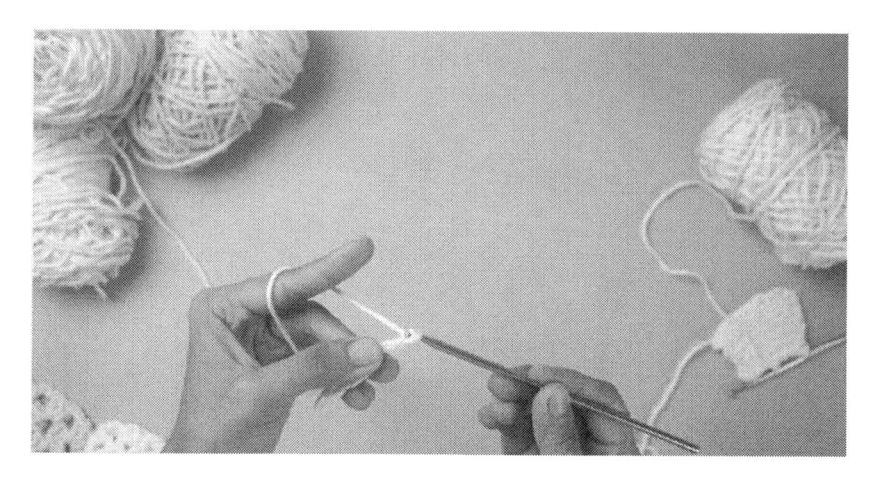

- **Method#2: The Knife Method**

Position your thumb such that it is either on the thumb rest or maybe just directly in front of it. Find the wide, flat piece of the crochet hook, also known as the thumb rest, and place the thumb of the hand that you use most frequently on this section of the hook. Put your thumb in front of the thumb support rather than on it if you want the fingertips to be closer to the center of the hook. This can be accomplished by moving your thumb.

    o There are crochet hooks available that include a flat part on both the front and the back of the hook. In order to manipulate the stitches, place the thumb on the side of the needle that has the loop pointed in your direction.

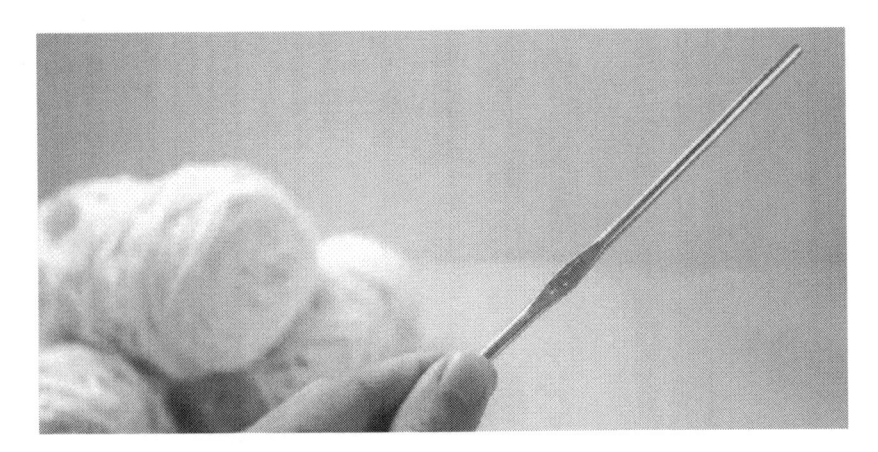

To get a better grasp on the hook's shaft, curl the other fingers over it. As soon as you have your thumb in the correct position, pretend that you are gripping a knife and allow your fingers to curve over the course of the hook. Don't tense up your hand in an effort to avoid overworking your muscles.

- o When you feel the beginnings of a cramp in your hand, consider relaxing your hold on the switching to the pencil grip.

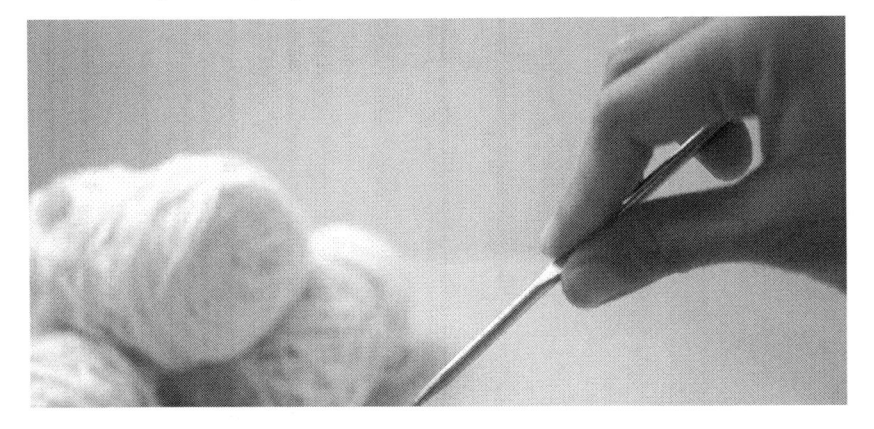

When you are crocheting, you can direct the motion of the hook by using your wrist. In contrast to the pencil approach, the knife method provides you with a more secure grip on the hook. This is an advantage if you have a tendency to crochet with a high level of tension.

- o You can purchase crochet handles that slip it onto a hook and function as a cushion if the constant brushing against by the hook has caused your fingers to get calloused.

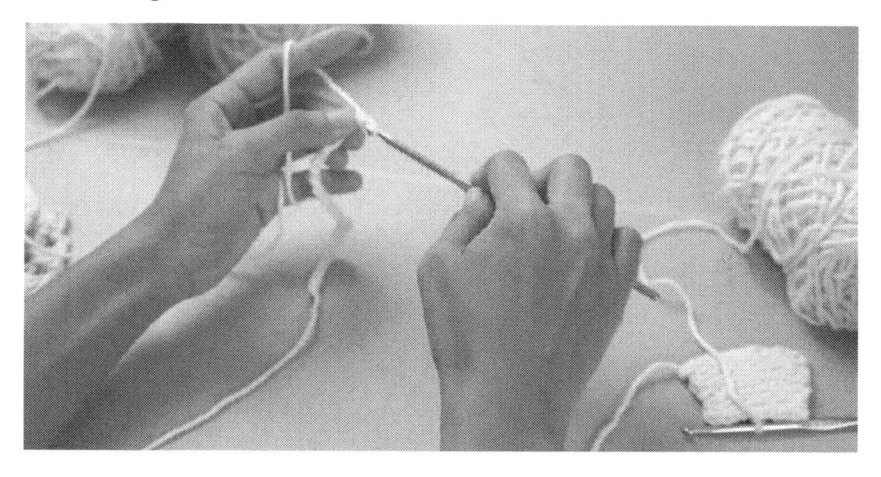

- **Method#3: Taking Hold of the Working Yarn**

When you are crocheting, you can direct the motion of the hook by using your wrist. In contrast to the pencil approach, the knife method provides you with a more secure grip on the hook. This is an advantage if you have a tendency to crochet with a high level of tension.

- o You can purchase crochet handles that slip it onto a hook and function as a cushion if the constant brushing against by the hook has caused your fingers to get calloused.

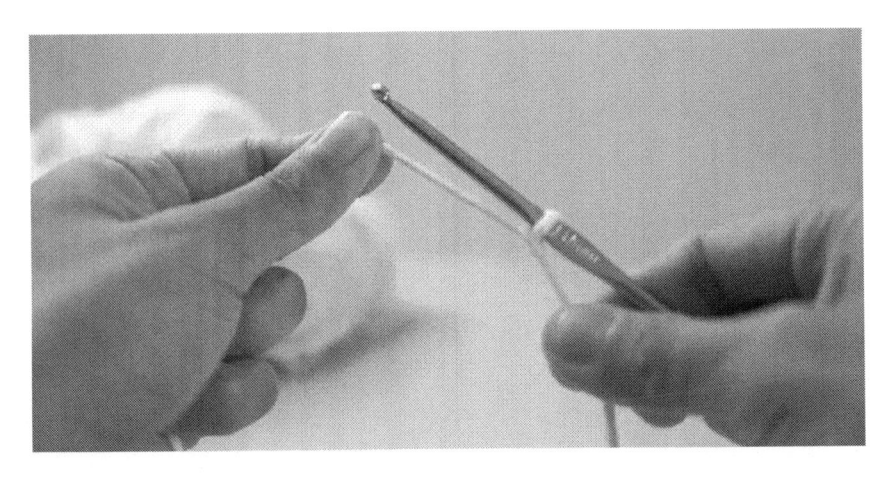

For the increased influence of the tension, twist the working yarn over the pinky finger of your other hand. Place the yarn you are working with beneath the pinky of the hand that is not your dominant hand and twist it once around the finger. The next step is to bring the yarn under your thumb by pulling it over your ring, middle, and index fingers before bringing it under your thumb.

- o Pull your hand together until all the fingers meet to increase the stress in the yarn. Spreading your fingers apart will help relieve some of the stress.
- o If the sensation of the yarn winding around your pinky causes discomfort, try placing it all under your pinky and pulling it up over the rest of your fingers instead. The next step is to place something under the thumb so that your hand can still handle the yarn, but none of your fingers will be entangled.

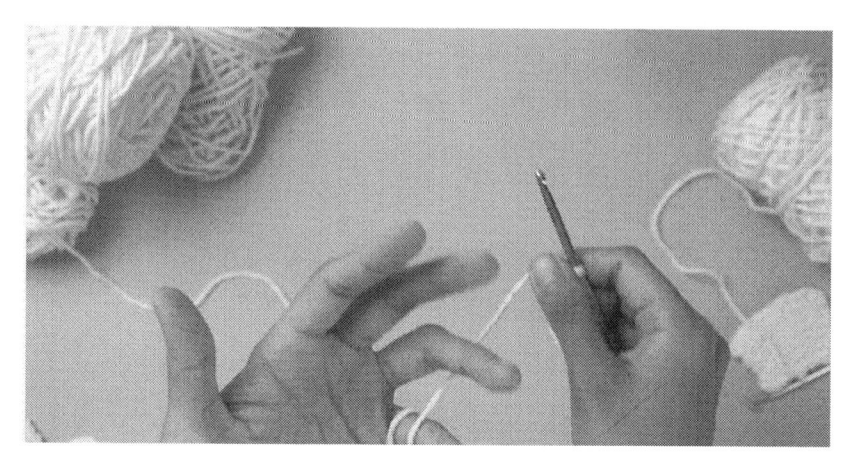

If you find that looping the yarn across your index finger makes the task more manageable, give it a shot. If you'd prefer to manage the working yarn with your index finger, move it under your pinky and above your ring and middle fingers. This will give you more room to work with your index finger. After that, loop the thread around the index finger on your dominant hand.

- o If you attempt holding the yarn in this manner, you'll be able to grasp the crocheted cloth with the thumb and middle finger instead of using your other fingers.

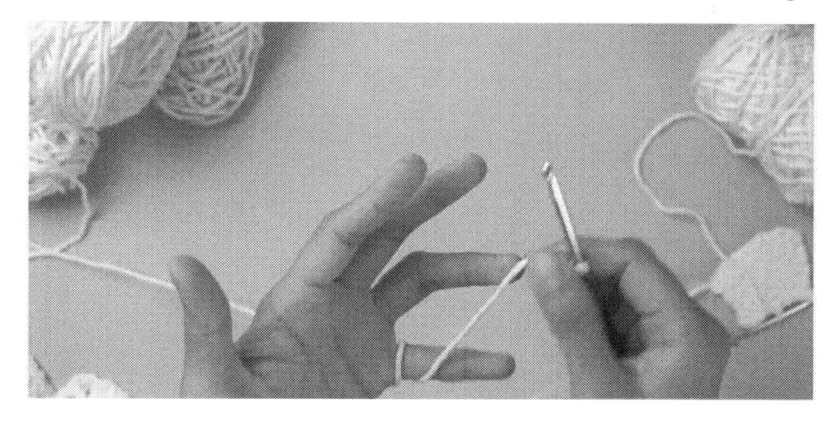

You can hold the yarn using a variety of different techniques, or you can come up with your own method. Experiment with each of these approaches and make adjustments to each one until you discover a method that suits you well and seems natural to you. One possible use for the yarn is to wind it around the ring and pinky finger of your left hand. You could even tie the yarn between your fingers and your thumb if you want to.

- o Keep in mind that there is no one right technique to handle the yarn as long as the method you choose is comfortable for you.

Chapter 4: Patterns

The chapter will provide in-depth information on various crochet patterns. Crochet patterns must be learnt efficiently if you want to become a pro in this art

1. Cable

Crossing stitches might be difficult to understand at first, but the cable stitch is a great way to ease into the process.

By working back across a set of stitches that you have previously knitted, you may create the optical illusion that the threads in your project are switching locations, much as you would while knitting cables. The formation of a bias in the fabric is prevented thanks to the horizontal columns of cables and the alternating rows of single crochet.

Stitch multiples of four plus two.

Step 2

Step 1: single crochet stitch in the second chain from the hook, 1 single crochet stitch in each chain until the end of the row, and turn.

Step 2: Chain 3, skip the first single crochet, *skip the next single crochet, 1 dc in each of the following 3 sc, 1 cable stitch; repeat from *, 1 dc in the starting chain.

Step 3

Step 3: Ch 1, skip the first double crochet, 1 sc in each remaining dc until the end of the row, 1 sc in the beginning chain, and turn.

Step 4 Repeat Steps 2–3. For the special stitch known as the cable stitch, work 1 double crochet by putting the hook 4 stitches to the right of the sc that was just skipped.

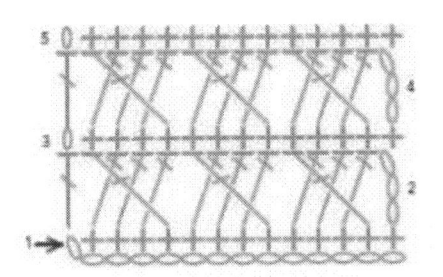

2. The Cabbage Patch (n.)

A row of stitches that look like cabbages has always been one of my favorite knitting patterns. This is a simple yet ingenious stitch that repeats itself every two rows. The double-crossed doubles that make up the first row each have two chains running through the center of them. This chain gap will be knitted into four double stitches in the following row. In addition to giving the cloth an intriguing texture, this also enables the fabric to be more robust.

Stitches in multiples of 4 plus 7

Step 1: Work four dc in the fifth loop from the hooks, then continue the following sequence until you have two chains left: *bypass three chains, work dc in the next chain*. Finish by skipping the last chain and dc'ing in the last chain until spinning.

Step 2

Step 2: Make a chain three, which This is equivalent to making two chains and a double crochet., then skip the first double crochet, *skip 3dc, 1dc in next dc, ch2, 1dc in first of skipped dc; rep from * to end, 1dc in tch, turn.

Step 3

Step 3: Chain 3, then work four double crochets in each space between chains 2 and turn.

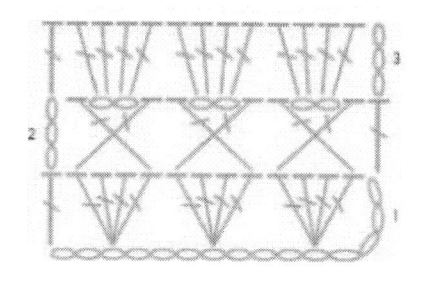

Step 4 Perform Steps 2 and 3 Once Again

3. Hot-cross Bun

The Hot cross Bun stitch has a few unique characteristics that make it intriguing. Because it is constructed using a three-row repetition, it is reversible and, as a result, is an excellent option for use in throws and blankets. If your project has rows of crossed trebles, it will develop rapidly. These rows of double clusters between the deep crossings provide a sense of equilibrium. This contributes to the overall design by adding more texture and intrigue. If you need to become more familiar with this stitch, it is recommended that you practice it with a cotton yarn of medium weight and light color when you first attempt it. When you have gained enough experience, this pattern works well with various yarn kinds, including some chunkier variations.

Repeat the sequence of three stitches plus two, plus one for the foundation chain.

Step 1 (WS) (WS) 1 sc in the second chain from the hook, 1 sc in each chain until the end of the row, and turn.

Step 2

Step 2: Make a chain of four (this counts as one triple crochet), skip the first single crochet, then work the following pattern as follows: *triple crochet over the next three single crochets*, repeat from * to the very last single crochet, then triple crochet in the very last single crochet and turn.

Step 3

Step 3

Step 3: Chain 4 (This is equivalent to making two chains and a double crochet.), *dc3tog in next ch-1 sp**, ch2; repeat from * until final rep is at **, ch1, work one double crochet in the fourth chain from hook, turn.

Step 4

Step 4: Chain 1, single crochet in the first stitch, single crochet in next chain, *1 sc in next cl, 1 sc in each of the following 2 chains; repeat from * to end, turn.

Step 4

Step 5 Repeat Steps 2–4.

TrX (Treble "X" shape worked over 3 sts): yo twice, insert hook in next sc, repeat the motion of pulling the loop through twice. 2 loops, skip next sc, yo, insert hook in next sc, yo, pull loop through, [yo, pull loop through 2 loops] 4 times, ch1, yo, insert hook halfway down st just made, yo, pull loop through, [yo, pull loop through 2 loops] twice.

4. The Numbers Zero and Crosses

Because the crossing doubles and chain spaces in this stitch appear precisely like the child's game, it was given the name Zeros and Crosses, which is extremely fitting. Like many others in this area, this stitch is based on a three-row repetition, and as a result, it may be worked in either direction. When it comes to producing wraps and scarves, this is a helpful feature. Because the top of the crossing stitch is thinner than the base, caution is required while arranging the two "legs" of the cross. This stitch would work well with a wide variety of yarn choices.

Perform multiples of 2 stitches plus one more stitch, adding 3 for the foundation chain.

Step 1 (RS) (RS) 1 double crochet in the sixth chain from the hook, *ch1, skip 1 chain, 1 double crochet in the next chain*, repeat from * to finish, turn.

Step 2

Step 2: Ch 3, skip the next chain space, *1dc in the next chain space, insert hook from behind dc just worked in ch sp skipped; rep from * to end working 1dc in the 4th of ch-4 and 1dc in the last ch, turn. Step 3: Ch 3, skip the next chain space. Step 4: Ch 3, skip the next chain space. Step 5: Ch 3, skip the next chain space. Step 6: Ch 3, skip the next chain space.

Step 3

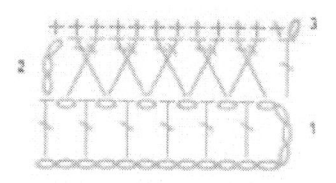

Step 3

Step 3: Chain 1, single crochet in the first stitch, single crochet in the next stitch and every stitch to the end of the row, finishing with single crochet in starting chain, turn.

Step 4

Step 4: Make a chain of four stitches (This is equivalent to making two chains and a double crochet.), skip two stitches, and then work one double crochet into the next stitch. Then, repeat the following pattern: *ch1, skip one stitch, and then work one double crochet into the next sc* until you reach the end of the row.

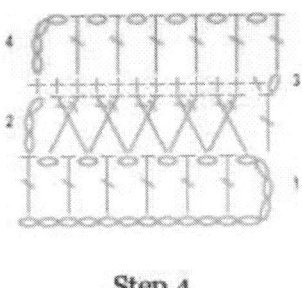

Step 4

Step 5 Perform Steps 2–4 once again.

5. Triangles Turned Inside Out

The construction of Inverted Triangles is similar to that of Little Pyramids; however, the triangles in Inverted Triangles are now broader and are worked in both directions.

To do this, knit a succession of larger stitches away from the chain length and then add a double treble between each triangle. This will provide the desired effect. Because the pattern is constructed on a three-row repetition, it may be carried out in either direction.

Stitch multiples of six plus two.

Step 1 (RS) (RS) 1 sc in the second chain from the hook, 1 sc in each chain until the end of the row, and turn.

Step 2: Ch 1, 1 sc in the first sc, *ch 6, 1sc in the 2nd ch from hook, 1hdc in the 3rd ch from hook, 1dc in the 4th ch from hook, 1tr in the 5th ch from hook, 1dtr in the 6th ch from hook, skip 5 sc (from the previous row), 1 sc in the next sc; repeat from * to the end, turn.

Step 2

Step 3: Chain 5 (this counts as 1 double crochet), work the following pattern: *1sc in the chain at the top of the next triangle, ch4, 1dtr in the next sc; rep from * till the end, turn.

Step 4: Chain 1, single crochet in each double triple crochet and single crochet group until the end of the row, working the last sc in a fifth of the chain-5 at the beginning of the row before turning.

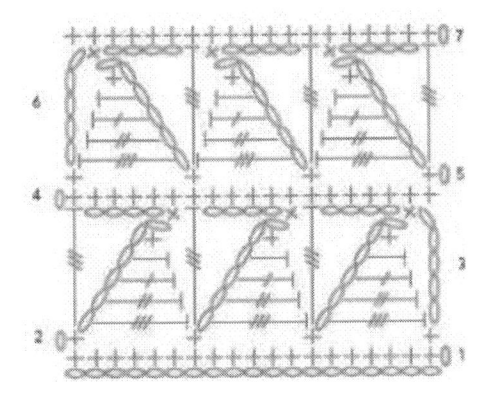

Step 5 Perform Steps 2–4 once again.

Chapter 5: Projects

1. Hairpin Lace Neck Scarf

YOU Will NEED

Yarn

- 95 yd (86 m) double knitting weight yarn
- Shown: Tilli Tomas Plie, 100% silk, 50 g/140 yd,

Gloxinia: 1 skein

Hooks/Tools

- G/4 mm crochet hook or size needed to obtain gauge
- H/5 mm cachet hook or size needed to obtain gauge

- Hairpin lace loom that will adjust to 4 W' (11 .5 cm)
- 5 clips on markers
- Tapestry needle

Gauge

- 36 Ips = 4" (10 cm) with 2 strands yarn and larger hook
- 16 sc = 4" (10 cm) with 1 strand yarn and smaller hook

Skill level

- Intermediate

Strips

Notes: Using two strands of yarn bound together and a 1 x 1 cable ioin, you may make six short strands of hairpin lace. Then, to make elaborate crochet edging, a single strand of yarn is joined at one of the short ends. The edging is continued without cutting all the way around the scarf's circumference.

Set up the loom with 4 Y2 prongs "(11.5") meters apart. Create six strips with 28 loops, each using double-stranded yarn.

Leave 8 "Starting and ending tails are 20.3 em.

Joins for Work Cable

Join two strips by following steps 1 through 3 on page 261. Consider each loop's two strands as one. With the last loop on your hook, complete the connection. Clip-on markers should be used to temporarily fasten this loop.

The fabric's RS is the side that is now facing you.

Join each of the next five strips to a free side of the linked piece while maintaining RS facing. Join these strips using the same technique as the previous join, temporarily anchoring the final loop on the hook with a clip-on marker.

Side Edging Short

Take a single strand of yarn and insert a smaller hook with the RS facing into the right- most loop on the shorter side (remember that each loop contains two strands!).

Working everything along into untwisted loops:

Row 1: Ch 4, tr in first 2-lp-grp, ch 2, 2 tr in same 2-lp-grp, [(2 tr, ch 2, 2 tr) in next 2- loop-group] 5 times, (2 tr, ch 2, 2 tr) in last 2-lp-grp, turn. (7 groups of loops worked) Row 2: Sl st in each of first 2 trs and in first ch-2 sp. Ch 1, sc in same ch-2 sp, [ch 2, (tr, ch 1) 3 times in next ch-2 sp, ch 2, (tr, ch 1) 3 times in same ch-2 sp, ch 2, sc in next ch-2 sp] 3 times, turn.

Row 3: Ch 3, [ch 3, (dc, ch 2, sc in last de) 5 times in ch-3 sp, ch 3, de in next sc] 3 times. Work ch 2, 3 sc in edge tr of Row 1, then continue to Edge Long Side.

Long Side Edge

A straightforward pattern of [ch-5, sc around one side (2 strands) of edge loop] is used to edge the long side. Scratch into each join as well as the middle stitches of each strip.

Stop and pull the chain firmly to ensure it is uniformly spaced around the edge of the strips as you go. To prevent the chain edging from puckering or ruffling, adjust the number of chains before working sc into the middle of the strip or the joins.

Work the last stitch to match the top of the strip on the neck scarf's opposite side.

Repeat the steps for Short Side Edging and Edge Long Side to edge the other short side of the strip. Work a chain and then a Sl stitch to the third chain at the beginning of Row 3 to finish this long side edge. Knot off.

Finishing: To imitate the join pattern, bind the end loops of each join to its beginning loops using tails. Trim all ends after weaving in.

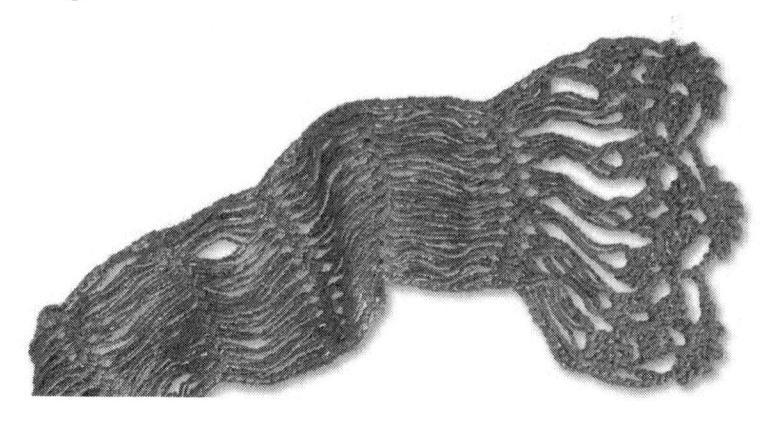

2. Broomstick Lace Jewelry Frame

YOU WILL NEED

Yarn

- Dk-weight yarn, 140 yd (129 m)
- Shown: Tilli Tomas Plie, 100% silk with beads, 50 g/140 yd (129 m), Jade: 1 skein

Hooks/Tools

- 3/D (3 .25 mm) crochet hook or size needed to obtain gauge
- US #19 (15mm) straight knitting needle
- Tapestry needle

Materials

- 11" X 14" frame or size frame desired
- Coordinating fabric
- Cardboard cut to fit frame
- Stapler

Gauge

- 25 sc = 4" (10 cm) (unstretched)
- Approx 20 sts = 4" (10 cm) in Broomstick Lace

Pattern (stretched)

Jewelry Frame

Specifications: This project needs a frame without glass that can hold knitted or crocheted fabric of a certain thickness.

Double crochet stitches are used in Stage 2 of this broomstick lace design row.

Ch 57, turn.

Basis (RS): Sc into the second chain from the hook and into each subsequent chain till the end.

Stage 1, Row 1: Extend the loop that is on the hook and slide it onto the knitting needle without twisting the work. There

~ 109 ~

will be 56 loops after inserting the crochet hook into each sc, pulling up a loop, and transferring it to the knitting needle without twisting it.

Stage 2, Row 1: Work 3 more dc in the same IPs, [4 dc in next group of 4 Ips] till the end of row — 14 clusters. Stage 2, Row 2: Work 3 more dc in the same IPs, [4 dc in next group of 4 Ips] until the end of the row. Never turn.

Stage 1, Row 2: Extend the loop that is on the hook and slide it onto the knitting needle without twisting the work. To transfer a loop to a knitting needle without twisting it, insert the crochet hook into each dc in the row before and draw up a loop. Pull up a loop at the top of the ch-3 to create the last loop.

Repeat Stage 2, Row 1 in Stage 2, Row 2.

Twelve times, or until the piece is long enough to fill the whole length of the frame, repeat Stages 1 and 2 of Row 2.

Knot off. Integrate ends.

Build the frame

A cardboard insert that has been trimmed to fit the frame opening is included with many frames. Make one out of thin cardboard if yours doesn't. Next, trim your fabric to a 1 "(2.5 cm) wider on all sides than the cardboard insert, and staple it to the cardboard as closely as you can to the edges all around.

The frame itself ought to conceal the staples. Because you'll be stapling your knit or crochet projects in the same method and want to avoid hitting the same staples, take note of where the staples are placed.

Variations

Any yarn may create a broomstick lace panel for any frame size. Make a 4 "To determine the stretched gauge, use a 10 cm square gauge swatch and stretch it vertically and horizontally. Take note of the horizontal distance. Based on the pattern stitch multiple, use your stretched gauge swatch to calculate the right number of stitches to meet your selected frame dimensions:

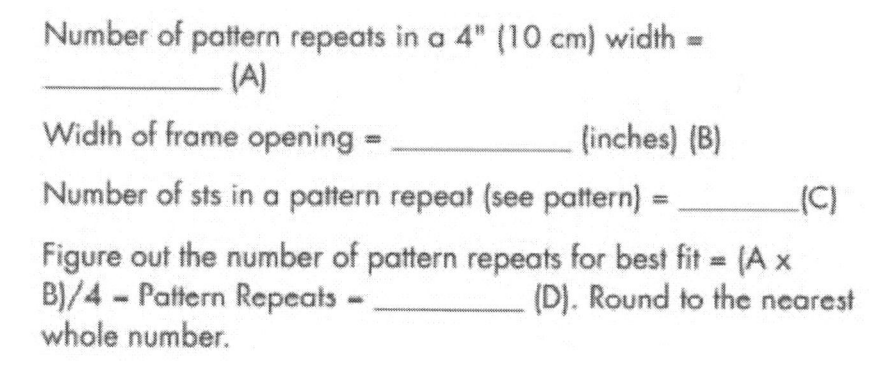

Number of pattern repeats in a 4" (10 cm) width = _____ (A)

Width of frame opening = _____ (inches) (B)

Number of sts in a pattern repeat (see pattern) = _____ (C)

Figure out the number of pattern repeats for best fit = (A x B)/4 - Pattern Repeats - _____ (D). Round to the nearest whole number.

Fit for length as you work: Using your stitch gauge, make sure that your project's width is a close match to the frame's width. Stop occasionally stitching to fit the work over the frame insert and gauge when sufficient rows cover the height of the frame aperture to get a perfect height. Once it reaches the required length, stop.

3. Freeform Handbag

YOU WILL NEED

- Scrambles
- ⅜ Yd (0.35 m) synthetic fleece for interlining
- ⅜ Yd (0.35 m) lining
- Needle and thread
- Yarn to coordinate with scrumbles
- Button

1. Shape the interlining by cutting it. Cut a piece measuring 9" x 15" (23 x 38 cm) and circle one end to use as the handbag pictured. Cut a piece of lining using the interlining as a reference, leaving ½" (1.3 cm) extra on edge.

2. Position the scrumbles, so their edges meet each other on the interlining; as little as possible should be left unfilled. Later, you may add more crochet stitches to close in the gaps. Attach the interlining with the scrumbles.

3. Use complementing lightweight yarn to stitch the scrumbles together, or use thread and a needle to attach them to the interlining. Add more crochet stitches to any empty places.

4. Sc around the full outer edge in a single row. Make a button loop in the middle of the rounded end.

5. Cover the bag piece's wrong side with the lining, right side up. Turn the edge under so that it just covers the interlining all around. Attach the lining with pins. Attach the bag's liner with sewing.

6. Fold the bag into the form of an envelope and stitch the side seams. Include a button. If desired, add a shoulder strap.

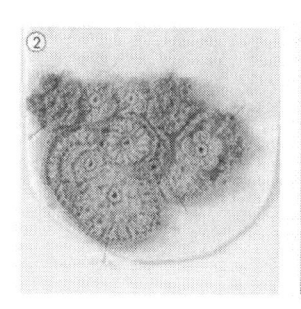

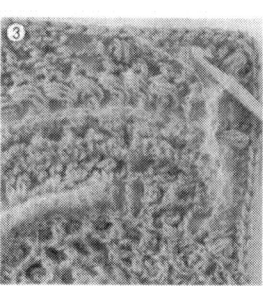

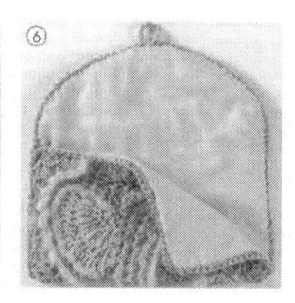

4. Polish Star Pillow

You Will Need

Yarn

- Worsted yarn [medium (4)] in two complementary colors, 6 oz (170 g) each

Hooks

- 9/1 (5.5 mm)

Notions

- stitch holder such as a safety pin
- tapestry needle
- 18" (45.5 cm) Square-shaped cushion

Gauge

- 12 sts = 4" (10 cm) and 6 rows = 4" (10 cm) measured over the stitch pattern given for the back of the pillow

Finished size

- Approximately 17 1/2 " (44.5 cm) square

Notes:

Extended double crochet, or edc, has the height of a triple crochet but without the additional twist, giving the stitch a softer appearance.

To make an Edc, begin by inserting the hook as you would for a regular double crochet. Then, bring the yarn to the front, so three loops are on the hook. Yo, draw through only the first loop, extending the stitch's height. Yo, pull through two loops twice. One created by Edc.

C 1: The first color successfully inserts a 4Edc between each loop of a loch.

C2: A group of 2Edc and 6Edc were used in the contrast color on alternating rows.

Front

In C 1, ch 51.

Row 1: Work 1 edc in the fourth ch from the hook, ch 10, *skip 1 ch, work 1 edc in each of the following 4 ch, ch 10, repeat from * to the final 3 ch, skip 1 ch, 1 edc in the next ch, and 1 edc in the last ch. Change to C2 when there are two loops left on the hook. Turn work. Work 11 groups of skips 1 st,

The pattern is formed by rows 2–5, inclusive. Rows 2 and 3 should also be repeated once more.

Link the 10-ch loops together to create the pattern before finishing the last row. Fasten C2 off.

CD

48Edc after accounting for the turning ch, 4Edc + two halves (1)

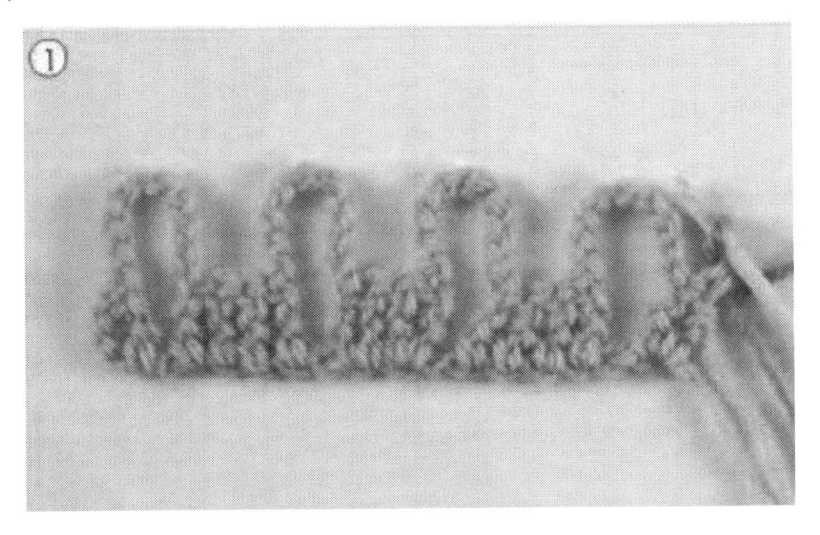

Row 2: Ch4, 2Edc in next st, ch 1 0, *skip 1 stitch, 1 Edc in next 2 stitches, ch 10, skip 1 stitch, (2Edc in next st) thrice, ch 10, rep from * to end, only inserting 1 Edc in final sl. Incorporate the hook's loop into a stitch holder. AVOID TURNING THE WORK (2).

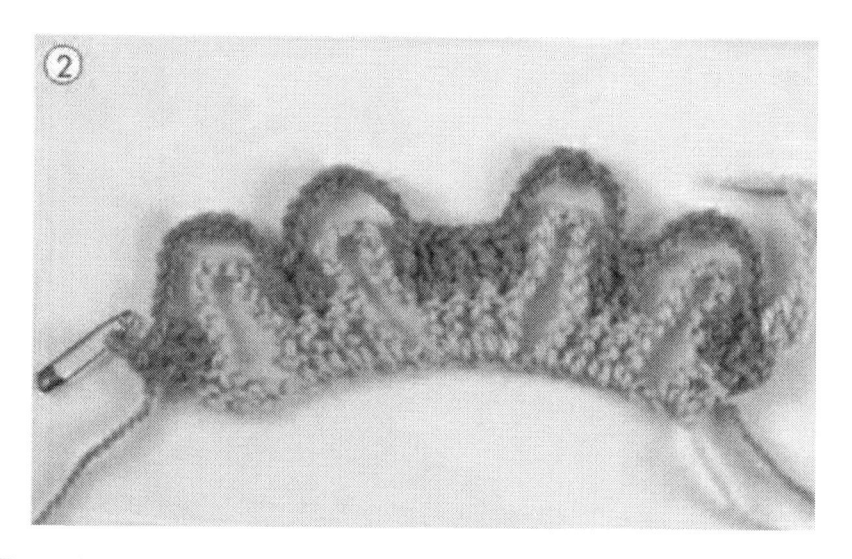

Row 3: Begin at the beginning of row 2 and thread the C1 yarn through the top turning ch. Then, ch 3, 1 Edc in the next stitch, skip one stitch, *ch 1 0, (2Edc in the next stitch) twice, ch 1 0, skip one stitch, 1 Edc in the next four stitches, skip one stitch, and repeat from * to the last 2-st group. Ch10, working the final stitch as follows: (2Edc in next st) twice, ch10, skip 1 st, 1 Edc in next st, 1 Edc in the last stitch. When there are just 2 loops of C1 left, change to C2 by inserting the hook, collecting the loop from the holder, and bringing it through both the loop and the stitch to secure the C2 loop from the previous row. Turn the work (3)

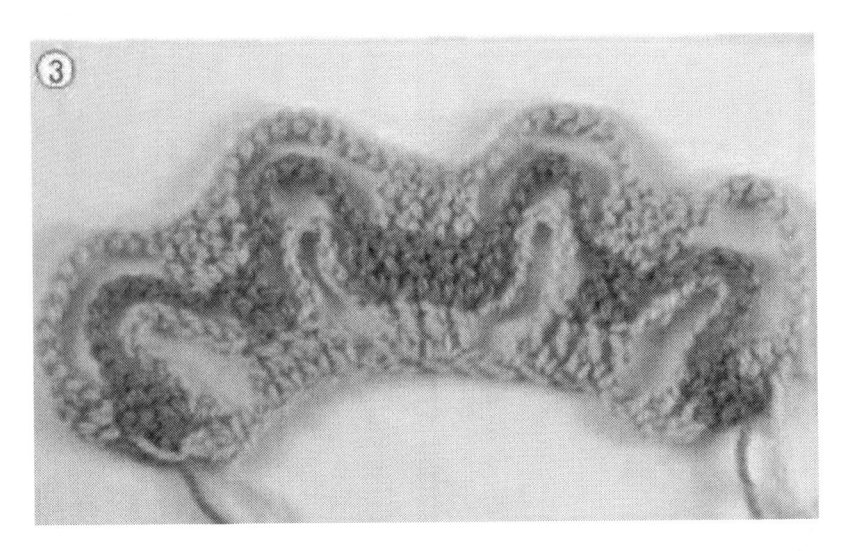

Row 4: Ch 13 (to serve as the first Edc), skip 1 stitch, *2Edc in the first stitch of the next group, 2Edc in the next 2sts, 2Edc in the last stitch of the group, ch 1 0, skip 1 stitch, 1 Edc in next 2sts, skip 1 stitch, repeat from * to last group of 4sts, 2Edc in the first stitch of next group, 2Edc in next 2sts, 2Edc in last

Row 5: Return to the beginning of the previous row and work with C 1, passing it through the third of the turning ch of the previous row, ch3, and one edc in the same space as the turning ch, *ch 10, skip one stitch, and then make two edc in the next stitch twice, repeating this pattern to the last group of six stitches, ch 1 0, skip 1 stitch, 1 edc in the next 4 stitches, skip 1 stitch, ch 1 0, and 2 edc in the final stitch to secure the loop in the holder as stated at the end of Row 3.

The pattern is formed by rows 2–5, inclusive. Rows 2 and 3 should also be repeated once more.

Link the 10-ch loops together to create the pattern before finishing the last row. Fasten off C2

Assembling the loops

1. The 10-ch loops of the odd-numbered rows (C 1), located on either side of the second group on the even-numbered rows, should always be worked first. Cross over these. Continue down the row.

2. To secure the crossing loops in place and create the "star" look, connect the 10-ch loops from the even-numbered row (C2) through each of them.

3. Connect the 10-ch loops in C1 by placing them just above the loops in C2 that you just linked.

4. Repeat steps 1 through 3 as necessary to connect all 10-ch loops once the C1 and C2 loops have been completed.

Connect the C1 loops across the 2nd group to achieve an all-over pattern. It prevents columns from growing out of the "stars."

Last Row: Ch3, 1 dc in next st, 1 dc in next two sts, *(ldc through the 10-ch loop and the next st) twice, 1 dc in next 6 sts, rep from * to last 4 sts, 1 dc in each of the final 4 sts, ensuring sure the C2 yarn is following the linking pattern as closely as possible. Cut the C 1 yarn. Securely sew all ends together.

Back

You can make the pillow's front and back identical. You could want a flatter cloth on the side that would be the least visible.

In C 1 ch51.

Row 1: 49 sts in the last ch, 2 dc in the last ch, 1 dc in each ch after that.

Ch1, *ch1, skip 1 stitch, 1 sc, rep from * to end, shifting to C2 in final sl. Row 2:

Row 3: Ch2, * 1 dc in the stitch of row 1 behind the ch-1 of row 2, 1 hdc in the next sc, rep from * to end.

Row 4: Ch 1, 1 sc in next st; repeat from * to last 2 sts; 1 sc in each of the next 2 sts; change to C 1 in the last sl.

Ch2, 1 HDC in the next stitch, *1 DC worked in the stitch of the row immediately below the ch-1 of the previous row, 1 HDC in the next sc, rep from *to the final stitch, 1 HDC in the last stitch.

Ch1, *ch1, skip 1 stitch, 1 sc; repeat from * to end; change to C2 in the last stitch. Row 6:

Row 7: Ch2, * 1 dc in the stitch immediately underneath the 1 ch, 1 hdc in the next sc, rep from * to end.

Row 8: Ch 1, 1 sc in next st; repeat from * to last 2 sts; 1 sc in each of the next 2 sts; change to C 1 in the last sl.

Rows 5 and 8 should be repeated ten times in total.

Ch1, 1 sc in each stitch till the end of the last row. Cut both yarns off.

Securely sew the ends together.

Alternative Extra

The sides of the Polish Star Stitch cloth may sometimes gape if it is attached to another piece of fabric or crochet after the loops have been linked. It is especially obvious when the Polish Star Stitch crochet has to be stretched, as in the case of a pillow cover when the pillow shell is smaller than its inner pad.

The next two-colour ribbon harmonizes with the Polish Star Stitch's two-color bands and the two-color bands on the reverse.

In (1 ch 6.

Row 1: Sc in the third chain from the hook and in each of the next three chains.

Row 2: (h2, 1 FPdc in the next stitch, 1 hdc in the last two stitches.

Row 3: (h2, 1 hdc in each stitch, ending with a (2 in the final stitch.

Repeat Row 2 in Row 4.

Repeat Rows 2 through 5 inclusively 5 times, and Rows 2 and 3 once. Row 5: Repeat Row 3, but change to (1.

Cut both yarns off. Securely sew the ends together.

Polish Star Stitch cloth was crocheted for the pillow's front; create two similar braids and thread them through the sides of the fabric. The easiest technique to ensure that the braid fills in any gaps is to thread them under the (1 chain loops) and over the (2 chain loops).

The chains worked in (1 need to lay over the (1 band of the braid, while the chain loops of (2 are concealed beneath the braid since the color bands need to coincide with both the back and front band's color.

To finish, use a large-eyed sewing needle and (1 if optional braids have been created and threaded through the sides of the Polish Star Stitch panel.

2. To create a pouch, join the back to the braids' sides and the cushion's top.

3. Place the pillow pad inside and single crochet the base of the crocheted pillow cover shut.

5. Bruges Lace

YOU WILL NEED

Yarn

- Patons Brilliant, 69% acrylic, 19% nylon, 12% polyester, 1.75 oz (50 g)/166 yd (152 m), 03005
- White Twinkle: 2 skeins.

Hook

- 5/F (3.75 mm)

Stitches used

- Chain
- Double crochet

- Unfinished double crochet
- Unfinished triple crochet

Gauge

- 10 rows of Bruges tape = 4" (10 cm)
- 4 dc = 3/4" (2 cm) but gauge is not important for this project

Finished size

- 5 1/2" (14 cm) wide and 66" (167.5 cm) long

Unusual abbreviations

- Unf dc = unfinished double crochet
- Unf tr = unfinished triple crochet

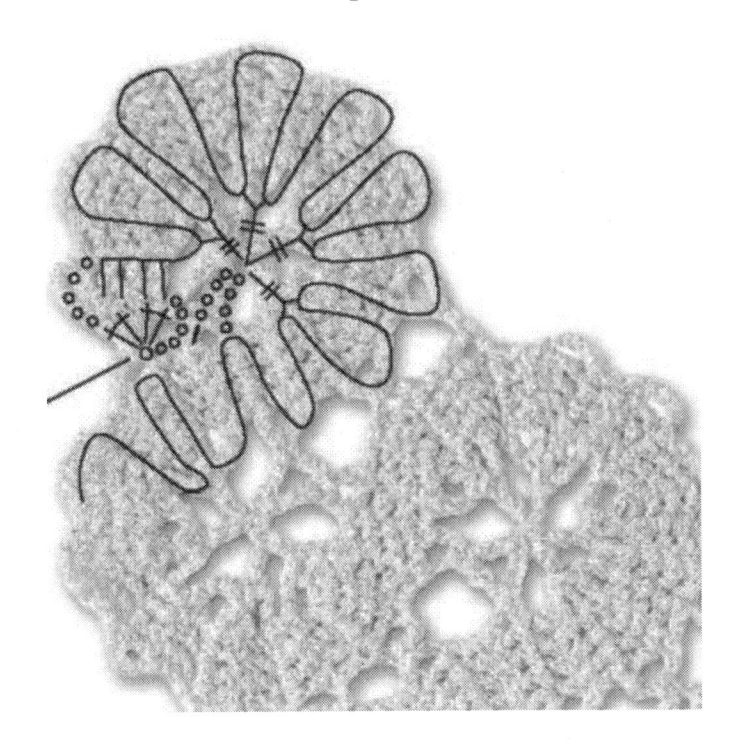

Ch6, 4 dc in the sixth ch from the hook in row 1, turn.

Rows 2 through 16 (tape rows): Ch 5 (arch), 4 dc in a row, turn (8 arches on each side of tape).

Ch2, place hook in adjacent arch, yo, draw through, yo four times, (insert hook in next arch, yo, draw through), repeat from row 2 to row 17 (joining row). [Yo, pull yarn through 2 loops twice]

Yo twice, [insert hook in next arch, yo, pull yarn through], 3 times (unf tr created). [Yo, draw across 2 loops] twice Rep from * to * three times (2nd unf tr formed), then once more with seven loops on the hook. Yo, draw through just three of the loops on the hook, [yo, draw through two loops]. Yo twice, draw through the last three loops, ch 2, turn, dc in each of the next four dc, turn (4 joining made).

Ch5, dc in each of the following 4 dc, turn. Rows 18, 20, (tape rows):

Row 19: Ch 6, sc in the middle of the preceding joining (between the second and third tr), ch 4, sc in the next free arch, ch 1, turn, 51 st into the second ch of the beginning ch-6, ch 2, dc in each of the following four dc, turn.

Row 21: Ch2, work 51 stitches, placing hook in first ch of Row 1 (beginning ch), ch2, turn, and dc in each of the next 4 dc.

Tape rows 22–33: Ch 5, dc in each of the next 4 dc, turn (6 arches outside the tape from last joining).

Rep Row 17 in Row 34.

Tape rows 35, 37, and 39: Ch 5, dc in each of the next 4 dc, turn.

Row 36: Ch 6, sc in the middle of the preceding joining (between the second and third tr), ch 4, sc into the next free arch, ch 3, turn, 51 st in the second ch of the beginning ch-6, ch 2, dc in each of the following four dc.

Ch2, sc into the opposite free arch, ch2, turn, and dc in each of the following 4 dc are the steps in row 38.

Row 40: Ch 2, dc into the opposing free arch, ch 2, turn, and dc in each of the next four dc.

Tape rows 41–50: Ch 5, dc in each of the next 4 dc, turn (5 arches outside the tape from last joining).

Repeat Rows 34–50 until the item is 66" (167.5 cm) long or the desired length.

Finishing

completing rows 34 and 35 of the rep.

Second row: Ch 6, sc into the centre of the previous joining (between the second and third tr), ch 4, sc in the following free arch, ch 1, turn, 51 stitches in the second ch of the beginning ch-6, ch 2, unf dc in each of the following 4 dc, yo, draw through all 5 loops on the hook, turn, 51 stitches into the opposite free arch. Trim off.

Snowflakes

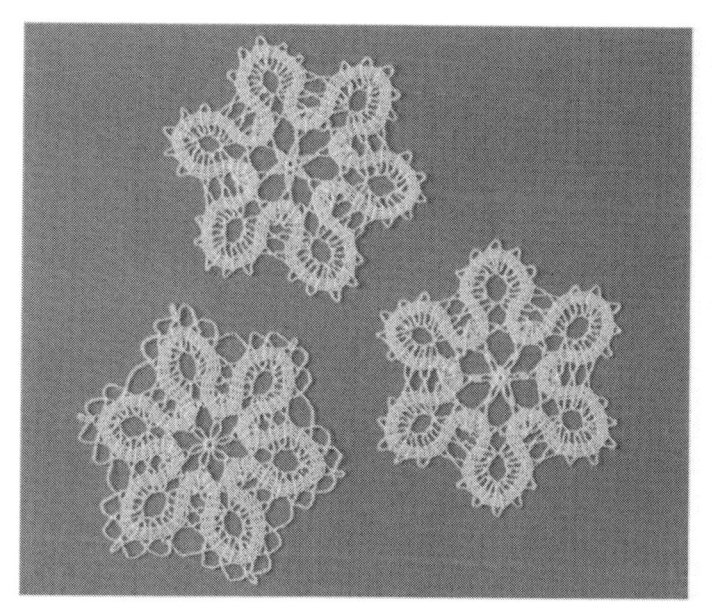

Conclusion

If you can't wait to start your project, you can pull the label off the skein of yarn you're going to use and then go right to work. Theoretically, it is possible to crochet with skeins of yarn, but in many instances, you will be able to obtain superior results if you wound the skein into a ball before beginning your project. This is particularly important to keep in mind for novices.

The following are some benefits that balls of yarn have over skeins: Avoid tangling. The ends of skeins of yarn wound using a center-pull method may quickly get tangled. The yarn in balls is less prone to get tangled.

Improve tension. Instead of working from a skein of yarn, you should consider working from a ball if you need help maintaining consistent tension.

There are machines called ball winders that may assist you with this process; however, you can also perform it by hand. Before you begin crocheting, comb through and secure your hair, especially if it is long enough to get in the way of your work. This makes keeping your hair out of the way as you work easier. Before beginning to crochet, it is recommended that you take off any jewelry you are wearing, particularly rings and bracelets. Your work will be slowed down if yarn gets caught on your jewelry.

When you are working on your crochet project, it is best to have no cats in the room with you. A moving ball of yarn is impossible for a cat to ignore. A cat's crochet creation may easily be undone with very little effort.

If you are crocheting at home while sitting in a comfortable chair, you can keep the ball of yarn on your lap or on the ground at your feet, whichever you find more convenient.

You want to ensure that the size of your stitches remains the same throughout the job. If you use different hooks, you risk confusing your audience. Problems arise even when switching between hooks of the same size made by different manufacturers.

If the stitches are too close together, try using a bigger crochet hook. Select a smaller crochet hook if the finished product is too loose. It is important to remember that the hook size specified on the yarn's label is only a suggestion of where to begin.

Before beginning a project, consider experimenting with different hooks. When you are already working on your gauge swatches is the best time to do this step. The manufacturers' hook sizes are usually different from one another. Slight variations in hook shape might cause you to adjust how you hold the hook and how you create your stitches.

Ergonomic crochet hooks are specifically designed to minimize hand and wrist strain. If you can track down an ergonomic hook you love using, you may discover that the time you spend crocheting is more pleasurable than it would have been otherwise. If you do not make the gauge swatch for your project, it will likely turn out to be the incorrect size. If you go back a few rows and see that you made a mistake, pull out the stitches you've done up to that point and start again.

There is no such thing as the "crochet police," and even if an experiment turns out badly, nothing terrible will happen to you. Experimentation and consistent practice are two of the most effective strategies to go beyond the beginning level. Consider these basic experiments: Make adjustments to the color scheme of a design; choose from a variety of yarns. Add or remove details: If you don't like the fringe that a design asks for, try substituting an edging instead, adding a flower to a simple hat, or as you gain more knowledge, you shouldn't be scared to do more difficult experiments:

Combine a solid color with vertical stripes; change up the stitches you use and get creative with your customizations: Alter a sweater with long sleeves rather than short ones and play about with the neckline. Not all of these experiments may be successful, but even the ones that fail will teach you something new.

Made in the USA
Monee, IL
10 August 2023